A-6 INTRUDER

D & S
VOL. 24

PART 1
BOMBER & TANKER VERSIONS

in detail & scale

D1613829

Bert Kinzey

TAB BOOKS Inc.
Blue Ridge Summit, PA 17214

Arms & Armour Press, Ltd.
Poole - Lane Cove - Johannesburg

This book is a product of Detail & Scale, Inc., which has sole responsibility for its content and layout, except that all contributors are responsible for the security clearance and copyright release of all materials submitted. Published and distributed in the United States by TAB BOOKS, Inc., and in Poole, Lane Cove, and Johannesburg by Arms and Armour Press.

CONTRIBUTORS:

Ray Leader	Joe Turpen
Flightleader	Grumman Aerospace Corporation
George Cockle	Grumman History Center
Jerry Geer	U.S. Navy
Wally Van Winkle	Public Affairs Office, COMNAVAIRLANT
Warren Munkasy	VA-85
Michael Grove	LT Robert Goodman, USN
Bill Curry	CDR David Stahlhut, USNR (Technical Advisor)
Mike Campbell	LCDR David McHenry, USNR (Technical Advisor)

Many photographs in this publication are credited to the contributors listed above. Photographs with no credit indicated were taken by the author.

FIRST EDITION
FIRST PRINTING

Copyright © 1987 by Detail & Scale, Inc.
Printed in the United States of America

Reproduction or publication of the content in any manner, without express permission of the publisher, is prohibited. No liability is assumed with respect to the use of the information herein.

Library of Congress Cataloging in Publication Data

Kinzey, Bert.
A-6 Intruder.

(Detail & Scale ; v. 24)
Produced with the cooperation of Detail & Scale, Inc.
1. Intruder (Bombers) I. Detail & Scale, Inc.
II. Title. III. Title: A6 Intruder.
UG1242.B6K52   1987   623.74′63   86-32142
ISBN 0-8306-8034-9 (pbk.)

Front cover: This colorful in-flight shot is of an Intruder from VA-65. The aircraft is carrying live 500 pound bombs.

(U.S. Navy)

Rear Cover: Cockpit in an A-6E TRAM.

(Grumman)

INTRODUCTION

This head-on view of an Intruder shows the almost triangular cross section of the large radome, the intakes, and stance on the landing gear to good effect. Multiple ejector racks are on the four wing pylons. (Cockle)

Grumman's A-6 Intruder certainly is not one of the most beautiful aircraft designs ever to come off of the drawing boards, but in terms of being able to perform the job for which it was intended, it may well be one of the best designs in military aviation history. The basic design of the attack versions of the Intruder have changed very little from prototype to the A-6E TRAM, which is the latest version flying. The new A-6F, which is still in the developmental stage, also retains the same basic Intruder airframe, with most advances being made internally. This illustrates that the Intruder's basic design was first rate from the start. In its combat use in Vietnam, and more recently in skirmishes with Libya, the A-6 has proven to be a capable performer. Detail & Scale is pleased to present this close-up detailed look at the Intruder, and this publication offers some interesting features that go beyond our usual coverage. CDR David Stahlhut, a naval aviator with time in the A-4, A-6, and A-7, has written a report that compares these three Navy attack aircraft. This provides an interesting and informative insight into these aircraft as seen from the pilot's point of view, and gives the reader a good understanding of the performance qualities of the aircraft. Detail & Scale is making every effort to include more of these "pilot's reports" in future volumes.

One of the highlights of this publication is the section written by Navy LT Robert Goodman. LT Goodman was the bombardier/navigator shot down over Lebanon in December 1983, and held captive for some time. LT Goodman writes about the mission that cost the life of his pilot, LT Mark Lange, and resulted in his captivity. He relates his inner feelings about being an American airman held prisoner in an undeclared war. This makes for most interesting reading, and is the first time LT Goodman has written such an account for a publication available to the public. LT Goodman also spent two days assisting the author in taking many of the detailed photographs in this publication, and his assistance and patience is greatly appreciated.

As always, the major focus of this publication is the many details of the aircraft, and most of the photographs in this book were taken specifically for this Detail & Scale volume. All bomber and tanker versions of the A-6 are covered from the prototypes to the A-6E TRAM. At press time, the A-6F had not been developed enough to be covered here. The EA-6A and EA-6B versions will be covered in a future volume. Every square inch of the Intruder is shown in greater detail than in any other publication. From the cockpit to the radar, from the wing flaps and spoilers to the equipment cage, and from the refueling probe to the tail hook, it's all here for the aviation enthusiast, historian, and modeler. The extensive number of detailed photographs will be especially helpful to the modeler, because there are so few models of the Intruder available, and all are rather old kits which lack detail and, with one exception, are of the older A-6A version. Our Modelers Section covers these kits, and provides a complete listing of decals available as of press time for this book. Also of interest will be our five-view scale drawings which were done especially for this publication by Dana Bell. We believe them to be the best drawings ever published of the Intruder.

Detail & Scale has taken over the Colors & Markings Series, and will publish a companion volume with this one. It will cover the colors and markings of U.S. Navy bomber and tanker versions of the A-6 since the Vietnam war. All Atlantic and Pacific squadrons are included. This Colors & Markings book will also be available from TAB BOOKS, Inc.

The A-6 is a truly remarkable aircraft when one considers its capabilities as an all weather attack aircraft. It has been, and will remain for some time to come, an important part of America's naval air arm. On the pages that follow, Detail & Scale is pleased to present the most detailed look ever published at yet another impressive aircraft from Grumman's famous "Iron Works."

DEVELOPMENTAL HISTORY

This is 147864, which was the first Intruder built. Several early features of the Intruder design that were later changed can be seen in this photograph. Most noticeable are the tail pipes that could be moved up and down to vary the direction of thrust through a twenty-three degree arc. In this photo they are in the down position. The original smaller rudder is visible, and the horizontal tail is in the original forward position. It has a fixed plane and movable elevator. Later it would be changed to an "all-flying" design. (Grumman)

The A-6 Intruder was born out of a need by the U.S. Navy for an aircraft that could attack ground targets in any weather, day or night. This need generated a Request for Proposals (RFP) in 1956, to which eight companies submitted no less than twelve design proposals. Grumman's design 128, which developed into 128Q, was the winning design, and a contract was issued on March 26, 1959. The aircraft was originally designated A2F-1, (A = attack, 2 = second type, F = Grumman's designator, and -1 = first version). The first flight took place on April 19, 1960, which preceded the public roll-out on April 28. In 1962, when aircraft designations were standardized, the A2F-1 became the A-6A.

The A-6 is a very sophisticated weapons delivery system as necessitated by the requirement to deliver ordnance in any weather, day or night, and to navigate without refer-

The large slot for the movable tail pipe is clearly visible in this banked view. This publicity photo demonstrates the large ordnance-carrying potential of the Intruder, although this load would not be practical for most combat conditions. External fuel tanks would most certainly replace some of the bombs. The aircraft is 147867, the fourth Intruder built. (Grumman)

ence to any external aids. By comparison, the A-7 Corsair II also is a sophisticated system, but its sophistication is aimed more at weapons delivery accuracy instead of all-weather capability.

After some understandable delays in getting all of the "black boxes" to work together properly, the A-6A joined both Navy and Marine attack squadrons. On carriers, one A-6 squadron was usually combined with two A-7 squadrons, but an exception of a dual A-6 wing has existed, as mentioned in LT Goodman's narrative later on in this book. Once deployed, the A-6 provided the Navy with an all-weather strike capability for the first time.

At the time the A-6 was designed, it was the aircraft carriers that had the responsibility for delivering the Navy's nuclear punch. Therefore the A-6, along with the A-3, A-4, A-5, and A-7, was designed to carry both nuclear and conventional weapons. But since that time ballistic missile submarines have taken over the role of delivering the Navy's nuclear weapons, particularly in the strategic sense. However, the carriers still maintain a nuclear striking capability, and the Intruder could be used as a nuclear bomber if needed. But its conventional ordnance load capability is also quite impressive, consisting of over three dozen types of ordnance from guided missiles to cluster munitions.

It is indeed unfortunate that the A-6 is not as popular or as well understood as many other modern combat aircraft. In commenting on the use of the A-6 over Lebanon when LT Goodman was shot down, the American press demonstrated a complete lack of understanding about the aircraft. One aviation photographer stated some time ago that he did not pay much attention to the Intruder because it was "ugly." Then he saw a flight demonstration by an Intruder, and it changed his mind! Certainly the A-10 Warthog has now made all other aircraft including the A-6 beautiful by comparison, but it is the Intruder's lack of eye appeal that has caused it to have a poor image in the minds of some people. It is appropriate here to take a closer look at the A-6 and reveal its true beauty.

The first Intruder, 147864, is seen here again with a number of modifications. The engines are now in a fixed position with the variable-direction thrust feature deleted. Note that there is only one boundary layer fence on each wing, and there are no speed brake fairings at the wing tips. The horizontal tail is fixed with an elevator and three fairings. There is no ECM antenna fairing on the tail. Also note the intake slot mounted on the intake just above the warning markings. *(Grumman)*

Any combat aircraft is actually a weapons system comprised of a multitude of components, all of which must work together in order for that aircraft to effectively deliver its weapons against a target. Very few people realize the complexity of a modern military aircraft. All they see when they look at one is the obvious aerodynamic design resulting from how the sheet metal skin was shaped over the skeleton of formers and spars beneath it. While they are at least subconsciously aware that also beneath that skin is a lot of electronics and plumbing, it is really the airframe's design that either impresses them or perhaps fails to impress them. If an aircraft appears sleek and fast, then it must be really super. If its lines are not so appealing to the eye, then many people seem to consider the aircraft less important and even less capable. These people probably try to pick out a new car the same way!

When a company that is in the business of designing and building aircraft begins to develop a new design, it must develop an airframe that will contain a large number of electrical components ranging from computers to radars, and from communications gear to navigational devices. There is the IFF gear, the flight control system, hydraulic system, and in most cases redundant systems to back up main systems. An engine, or engines, designed and built by another company for use in several aircraft, must be fitted into the airframe design along with sufficient fuel to feed them and enough airflow through intakes to provide the necessary air for the proper operation of the installed powerplant. While taking all of this under consideration, the designers must also try to meet any number of

performance criteria established by the service that will be the buyer of the aircraft. This criteria usually includes minimum standards for speed, range, ceiling, ordnance carrying capability, as well as take-off and landing distances. In the case of an aircraft that will operate from carriers, the demands are much more involved. With all this in mind, the designer must end up with an airframe that has good flight characteristics and is aerodynamically sound. It is no easy task! It must also be remembered that all of those internal components around which the airframe is wrapped are manufactured by companies other than the major contractor for the aircraft, and that these components are not designed to fit into this specific aircraft, but into several aircraft. Realizing all of this, one can begin to realize the problems in designing a modern military aircraft.

There are many things that can effect the capabilities or obsolescence of the design of a given airframe, but basically there are two things that can happen that will bring the end of a given design, removing it from the skies and relegating it to aviation history. The first of these happens when the design of the airframe can no longer perform to the standards necessary to survive in the combat in which it is expected to fight. This is perhaps most evident in fighters. When a fighter can no longer turn with or fly as fast as the adversaries it is likely to face, somebody starts screaming for a better aircraft. A good example of this is when the straight wing designs of aircraft like the F9F Panther and F-80 Shooting Star simply would not allow further increases in performance even with more powerful engines. Thus fighters with the standard straight wing design passed into the history books as new designs were found.

But this also applies to a lesser degree to attack aircraft. The basic flying qualities of the aircraft must be such that it can survive in combat, and its flight characteristics must be such that it can continue to be flown with newer weapons that it will be required to carry.

The second thing that will spell the doom of an existing

The A-6A was the first production version of the Intruder. Several changes from the aircraft in the photo above are noteworthy. Note the two boundary layer fences on each wing and the hinge fairings for the wing tip speed brakes. There is a large RHAW antenna fairing on the vertical tail, and the horizontal tail is an "all-flying" design rather than having an elevator. The in-flight refueling probe is now present, as is a light on the leading edge of the vertical tail. *(Grumman)*

airframe design is when that design will no longer accept the ever improving weapons delivery systems that continually upgrade the performance of the aircraft. Could the systems installed in the A-7 ever be forced to fit in an A-4? Yet the two aircraft were designed to perform the same mission, that of clear weather day attack and close air support. Likewise, could the systems in the F-15 Eagle fit into an F-86, or those in the F-14 Tomcat fit into an F11F Tiger?

There may also be new equipment added to perform new tasks. At the beginning of the war in Vietnam, few U.S. aircraft had any internal ECM or RHAW gear. By the end of the war they were loaded with it! So the airframe must not only take upgraded equipment over what may have originally been installed, but it may also be required to take entirely new systems. Thus it is evident that for an airframe design to be successful over a period of years, it must have outstanding flight characteristics and be able to adapt to the rapidly changing world of weapons delivery systems, avionics, and all of those other "black boxes" that occupy its internal spaces.

Time is usually one of the yardsticks used to determine the relative success or failure of almost anything man develops. Is something a "flash in the pan" or does it "stand the test of time?" Certainly, some military aircraft soldier-on beyond their useful life because economic or political constraints prevent building a replacement. But the major factor determining how long an airframe design will remain in operational service with little or no changes being made to its original form is how good that design was in the first place. While much has been written about the Intruder's outstanding all-weather weapons delivery capabilities, which are indeed truly exceptional, the basic design of the aircraft itself is no less superior. If the first Intruder built, (pictured on page 4 and again on page 5) is compared to photographs of the newest A-6E TRAM, very little change in design can be discerned. Most changes that were made were accomplished early in the flight test program as Grumman and the Navy "rung out" the design. Most noticeable of these changes were the deletion of the movable engine exhausts, enlarging the rudder, changing the horizontal tail from one with an elevator to one of an "all flying" design plus, moving it aft sixteen inches, elimination of the fuselage speed brakes, and addition of wing tip speed brakes. A second boundary layer fence was added to the wing, and later the covering was removed from the "Y" part of the tail hook. An ECM antenna fairing was added to the tail, but all of these changes were quite minor. By the time the first A-6A entered service, the design was finalized to such an extent that no further airframe changes of any consequence have been made. This permitted the use of many A-6A airframes to be converted to A-6Es, and while the A-6A remained in service after this conversion began, it was impossible to tell an A-6A from an A-6E even by looking at the BuNo. on the tail!

Many of these aircraft have been further modified to A-6E TRAM standards with relatively little effort. The A-6F,

The KA-6D tanker version of the Intruder deletes the all-weather attack capability in favor of tanker equipment utilizing the probe and drogue in-flight refueling system. It is now the Navy's standard carrier-based tanker.

(U.S. Navy)

which has yet to be finalized, also has some changes to the present Intruder design, but it is said A-6Es will be converted to A-6Fs, and this indicates that the design will still primarily be the well known tadpole shape of the Intruder that has existed for years.

After serving for over twenty-five years, the design of the Intruder has "stood the test of time," and proves the real worth and cost-effectiveness of a sound airframe design. By updating the avionics inside the aircraft, the aircraft has been improved considerably from the A-6A to the A-6E TRAM simply by updating the radar, avionics, computer, and other internal components. Essentially the Intruder has replaced itself as a newer, more capable attack aircraft, and is about to do so again in the form of the A-6F.

Since the A-6 was designed to be an attack aircraft, one of the primary considerations had to be the ability to lift heavy loads of ordnance and carry them a long way. While heavily loaded, the aircraft would still have to have good flight characteristics. Since the Intruder did possess good flying qualities when heavily loaded, it seemed logical that it could also be loaded with something other than ordnance. Thus, two versions of the A-6 were developed to perform missions other than the original all-weather attack role. One of these was the KA-6D tanker version. However, this required no major airframe changes. In fact, all KA-6Ds began life as A-6As, and were converted. The all-weather weapons delivery system was deleted, and the aft equipment cage was replaced with an in-flight hose and reel refueling system. In the tanker configuration, the aircraft carries five external tanks plus internal fuel. So by replacing ordnance with fuel, the Intruder became the Navy's primary tanker aircraft.

The second different role for the A-6 was that of electronic warfare. First came the EA-6A, which, like the KA-6D, was modified from existing A-6A airframes. The four-place EA-6B Prowler is the only real departure from the basic Intruder design, but demonstrates the flexibility of the design in meeting an entirely different requirement. The EA-6 versions will be the subject of a future Detail & Scale volume.

The finalized Intruder design as an attack aircraft, which was embodied in the A-6A, is comprised of an aluminum fuselage with a large bulbous radome at the nose, and a tapering design back to the tail. Length is fifty-five feet, nine inches. The mid-wing configuration has a twenty-five degree sweep at quarter chord, and a span of fifty-three feet. The wing area is 528.9 square feet. The horizontal tail is mid-mounted on the fuselage, and has a thirty degree sweep at quarter chord and a surface area of 117 square feet. The vertical tail is 79.25 square feet including the rudder with a twenty-eight degree sweep at quarter chord. None of these features have changed throughout the entire series of the attack versions of the A-6. Likewise, all attack and tanker versions have been powered by the J52-P-6 or J52-P-8 turbojet engines. The pair of -P-8 engines provide some 18,000 pounds of thrust, and have no afterburners. Internal fuel capacity is 15,940 pounds, and up to 8,020 additional pounds may be carried in external wing tanks.

It should be evident from the preceding discussion that the A-6 has one of the best mission-designed airframes ever built. But into this airframe must be placed the equipment that will allow it to perform its difficult role of all-weather bombing. With the A-6, this equipment was known as DIANE, which stood for Digital Integrated Attack and Navigational Equipment. Early promotion for DIANE included the cockpit display which was called a "highway in the sky." This "highway" allowed the crew to fly an entire mission, including attacking a target with a variety of weapons by any number of attack profiles, then return home without ever looking outside of the cockpit. The crew could change targets in the middle of the mission, or alter the attack profile over the target in the middle of the mission if desired. The Intruder could perform any needed navigation without the use of any external aids. The aircraft was designed to operate on single-plane missions, in pairs, or in larger flights. Two radars were installed in the A-6A, including the AN/APQ-92 search radar and the AN/APQ-112 track radar. These were replaced with the AN/APQ-148 multi-mode radar in the A-6E.

The DIANE system allowed the Intruder to operate over Vietnam in weather that grounded all other aircraft. This ability contributed to its low loss rate in combat. However, this new sophisticated equipment also provided its share of maintenance headaches, particularly at first, and resulted in a rather poor aircraft availability rate which has since been improved.

The A-6B and A-6C versions were modified from A-6A airframes, the -B being configured to perform the air defense suppression mission with anti-radiation missiles, and the -C being fitted with electro-optical sensors to detect targets not detectable by radar or visually. More information on these two versions is provided on pages 49 through 51.

Rather than writing a lengthy explanation about the internal changes that constituted the major differences between the attack and tanker versions of the Intruder, the following main differences table from the Navy flight (NAT-OPS) manual summarizes these differences. Numbers with AFC prefixes are airframe change numbers. During the life of an aircraft, changes are continually made to the airframe. These changes are given numbers, and the item in the column on the left began with the airframe change for the A-6 version indicated. If all examples of a given version of the A-6 had a certain feature, then an X appears in the appropriate column rather than an AFC number.

Throughout the remainder of this book, the different versions of the bomber and tanker versions of the Intruder will be studied in more detail. Differences as well as similarities between the versions will be illustrated with a great many photographs. For the enthusiast, these photos will tell the story of the Intruder far better than words or an alphabet soup of designations and terminology. However, additional data will be provided for each version. Suffice it to say here that even after a quarter-century of service, only the Air Force's F-111 is in the same class as the A-6 as an operational all-weather weapons delivery system. With the forthcoming A-6F, the Intruder will be around for many years to come. This is a truly remarkable record of an outstanding aircraft in a time of rapid change. It is unfortunate that the uninitiated public, and even some aviation buffs and photographers, don't give the Intruder much of a second look because it is not the most exciting looking airplane on the ramp. They are failing to realize that in the case of military aircraft, beauty is more than just skin deep.

MAIN DIFFERENCES TABLE

	A-6A	KA-6D	A-6E	A-6E TRAM [1]
20 KVA GENERATORS	X	—	—	—
30 KVA GENERATORS	—	X	X	X
MK-GRU-5 EJECTION SEATS	X	X	—	—
MK-GRU-7 EJECTION	AFC 119	AFC 119	X	X
BACK-UP HYDRAULIC SYSTEM	AFC 183	AFC 183	X	X
THREE POSITION CANOPY SWITCH	AFC 185	AFC 185	X	X
APCS AN/ASN-54 (V)	AFC 199	AFC 199	X	X
ACLS AN/ASW-25 (MODE II)	AFC 230	AFC 230	—	—
BALLISTICS COMPUTER AN/ASQ-61A	X	—	—	—
GENERAL PURPOSE COMPUTER AN/ASQ-133	—	—	X	—
SEARCH RADAR AN/APQ-92	X	—	—	—
SEARCH RADAR AN/APQ-148	—	—	X	—
TRACK RADAR AN/APQ-112	X	—	—	—
INERTIAL NAVIGATION SYSTEM AN/ASN-31	X	—	X	—
NAVIGATION COMPUTER AN/ASN-41	—	X	—	—
VIDEO TAPE RECORDER AN/USH-17 (V)	—	—	X	X
PROVISIONS FOR LB-31A STRIKE CAMERA	AFC 256	—	—	—
ADDITIONAL AIR CONDITIONING	—	—	—	X
ACLS (MODE I)	—	AFC 161	AFC 161	X
RECONFIGURED CNI	—	—	—	X
CAINS AN/ASN-92	—	—	—	X
GENERAL PURPOSE COMPUTER AN/ASQ-155	—	—	—	X
SEARCH RADAR AN/APQ-156	—	—	—	X
DRS AN/AAS-33 PROVISIONS	—	—	—	X
CONDOR AGM-53	—	—	AFC 344	X

[1] A-6E 159895 AND ON AND A-6E MOD M121 AND ON

VIEWS OF AN ATTACK PILOT

The A-7 and A-6 have equipped the attack squadrons of the Navy for many years. In an interesting narrative, Navy Commander Dave Stahlhut compares these two aircraft and the A-4 Skyhawk. He has considerable flight time in all three types.

(Cockle)

When Bert Kinzey asked me to write about the A-6 Intruder, I had serious doubts as to the appropriateness of anything I might relate. But he convinced me that based on my experience in various attack aircraft including the A-4 Skyhawk, A-7 Corsair II, and the A-6 Intruder, that my comparison of these aircraft from the pilot's point of view would make interesting reading for aviation enthusiasts. Hopefully, I can provide some insight into each of those Naval aircraft, and point out those attributes of the Intruder that have made it a most valuable attack aircraft for the U.S. Navy. I have flown the A-6C, KA-6D, A-6E, and A-6E TRAM configured versions of the Intruder, but it should be remembered that I am not a test pilot or aerodynamics engineer. Rather I am just an average naval aviator with experience in each of the aircraft. Since this book is on the A-6, most of my comments will relate to that aircraft.

Navy pilots have enjoyed a long love affair with the A-4 Skyhawk, and the reasons are many. The aircraft is simplicity personified. It is inexpensive, easy to repair, has manual backups for hydraulic and electrical systems, is reliable, and, considering when it was designed, is a very effective and accurate weapons system. The bottom line is that it is truly a "FUN" airplane to fly. Nimble and quick, it is one of the most responsive and maneuverable aircraft built. With the more powerful engines installed in the later versions, it is really an impressive airplane as those who have seen the Blue Angels perform in them can attest. Its primary role today is with Training Command, and it is also used as an adversary aircraft fighting against F-14s and F-18s. Its limitations are lack of range, limited weapons loadout, and no all-weather capability. Its retirement, though inevitable, is

sad, none-the-less.

The A-7E Corsair II, now being phased out by the F/A-18, is a most impressive day/VFR attack and CAS (close air support) aircraft. The A-7B was little more than a redone A-4 with improved range and weapons carrying capabilities. The A-7 does have an air-to-air capability, but its lack of power, poor turn radius, and tendency to depart in a high G, cross control situation, makes it less than desirable for that mission. The addition of the Gatling gun, and more recently, automatic maneuvering flaps in the A-7E, have greatly improved its air-to-air and CAS capabilities. The arrival of the A-7E was also a quantum leap forward in avionics and air-to-ground weapons delivery. In its era, it was second to none in accuracy. Reputed as a 10 mil bomber, the integration of the HUD, computer, and inertial systems made the aircraft indispensable in Vietnam, and more recently in Grenada. But the Corsair II also had some serious limitations. These included chronic engine problems, limited range and acceleration characteristics, especially when loaded with ordnance, and limited all-weather and night strike capabilities. Even more important may be the extremely high work load for the pilot in a combat environment. Some experts have estimated that to fly the A-7 to its capability in combat takes 1.7 men! As an amusing anecdote, after watching the movie "TOP GUN," a career A-7 pilot lamented that he would spend his entire naval career flying a "slug" compared to the other aircraft currently available. This is a rare admission from a "single seat" attack pilot. Although the jury is still out, the A-18, despite its sleek looks, tremendous G capability, and great speed, will prove a poor substitute for the A-7E. Its range

and weapons carriage limitations will so overshadow its 6 mil accuracy that the Navy will wish they had the A-7 back.

It is not the intent here to belittle the Corsair II. Its combat survivability and accuracy alone upholds its value to the carrier navy. This review merely points out relative strengths and weaknesses, especially when we begin to look at the Navy's only true all-weather attack aircraft -- the A-6 Intruder.

I've already stated that the A-4 was the most "fun" aircraft, and the A-7 the best day/VFR bomber I've flown, but the A-6E Intruder is the most impressive aircraft of the three. Hardly the most beautiful airplane in the sky, its design has given it exceptional range and payload, while maintaining excellent maneuverability, stability, G limitations, and an accuracy that is second to none in an all weather aircraft.

The A-6 was built under the "barn door" theory of aerodynamics. This theory basically states that if you design an aircraft that has the drag characteristics of a barn door, then no matter how much ordnance you hang on the airplane, the performance remains virtually constant. As you look at the A-6, you might be surprised to know that it is not the large nose radome that limits the aircraft's speed, but the wing design instead. The nose is actually quite efficient. It is the large thick wing, capable of carrying tons of stores and still have Gs available, that is the limiting factor.

The aircraft is also one of the few, if not the only, tactical jets that can be flown with the canopy open. Although not really a "goggles and scarf" airplane, you can open the canopy below 250 knots if the ejection seats are saftied. This is occasionally done on Post Maintenance Check Flights. With the canopy open and a little negative G, you can quickly and effectively vacuum out the cockpit of any debris, as well as any personal belongings if you are not

Above: With leading and trailing edge flaps on the wings, and with wing tip speed brakes, the Intruder is very stable at slow carrier-approach speeds. Engines are very responsive, allowing precise control. (Cockle)

careful.

The A-6 has reliable and powerful engines which provide great acceleration and climb characteristics as well as high speed at low altitude. If you look at the performance charts, you will find that the A-6E has the same climb and acceleration at military power as the F-14 at military power. This power allows the crew to fly a heavy ordnance mission at low altitude and a speed of better than 480 knots. With a configuration of twenty-two 500 pound bombs and a centerline drop tank, the A-6 is still a stable, responsive aircraft. The Intruder is also ideal in the carrier environment. The aircraft is very strong, and comes aboard at relatively slow speeds. The nearly instantaneous power response allows quick, precise, and effective corrections to be made "on the ball" as well as providing excellent go-around capability.

The A-6 was designed to be flown on single aircraft missions, day or night, and in all types of weather over any type of terrain. There may have been some question as to the early A-6 model's capabilities to achieve this, especially in the area of weapons system reliability. The A-6E, and more recently the A-6E TRAM, with its greatly improved systems that utilize the latest in solid-state electronics, has significantly enhanced the already awesome capabilities of the weapons system. I can remember one practice ordnance delivery mission where we took off at night in IFR weather, flew to the target, did multiple deliveries including low altitude laydown, loft, and over-the-shoulder bombing, then returned home not having once seen the target visually or even having been in VMC conditions the entire flight.

Above: No matter how much in the way of external stores is hung on the Intruder, its performance characteristics are quite good. This A-6A is loaded with twelve 500 pound bombs and three 300 gallon fuel tanks. (Geer)

This is hardly anyone's idea of a fun evening, but it is fully within the capability of the A-6 and its crew. Aside from being a 100 ¼ capable airplane, it can internally generate a GCA approach to any suitable field without the benefit of navaids. The A-6 can also fly a fully coupled automatic carrier approach in zero/zero conditions. The aircraft is an effective visual dive and pop-up bomber. The newer and faster computer in the TRAM update gives the A-6 a weapons delivery accuracy approaching that of the A-7E.

I could go on for paragraphs telling "sea stories" and extolling the virtues of the Intruder. It is sufficient to note the recent use in Libya. Used along with the F-111F, it was very highly effective in night strikes against various land targets using a variety of weapons. The marriage of the A-6 and the Harpoon missile system proved itself well, being totally effective against Libyan patrol craft. In each case the Intruder proved highly successful, and returned without loss. It should be noted that the only tactical aircraft not exported in any form is the A-6 Intruder, and for good reason.

It is only fair to mention the Intruder's limitations and drawbacks -- no airplane is perfect. Most of the shortcomings occur in the ACM/DCM environment. Although highly maneuverable with good G capabilities and an excellent turn radius, the A-6 is stiff on the controls, normally requiring the pilot to lock up the throttles and fight with both hands on the stick. The aircraft suffers from poor visibility to the lower rear quarters, and to the right for the pilot. It is essential that the B/N be well versed in DCM maneuvers, keeping a sharp lookout and making the proper calls to the pilot. This is no easy task. The aircraft has no effective forward-firing air-to-air capability. There is no gun (use of gun pods was discontinued years ago) and although I have fired a Sidewinder from the A-6, carrying it means you must give up a wing pylon that could be used for other ordnance. Therefore the aircraft rarely carries air-to-air missiles, and relies on fighter cover and its ability to "bug out" low and fast while using terrain to mask its exit.

The aircraft has suffered some wing stress problems, and efforts are being made to correct that. The lack of command ejection has, over the years, cost lives, and has resulted in some extraordinary and unusual attempts to save one's crewmember when he was disabled. This has long been a sore spot for some crews. The good news is that many of these areas where the Intruder needs improving are being addressed in the design and production of the forthcoming A-6F.

In summary, the A-6 Intruder combines an optimum mix of range, power, ordnance load, and delivery accuracy. Additionally, the aircraft is comfortable, roomy, forgiving of error, and nearly impossible to spin. Its strongest point may very well be its crew compliment. The side-by-side seating allows for effective crosschecking and closer personal contact. The work load is evenly distributed, and allows for mutual support and cooperation. Crews normally pair off for major cruises, and meld into finely honed teams. Each one knows the others strengths and weaknesses and compensates accordingly. I have yet to see the degree of respect and mutual support in any other type of two-place aircraft that I have seen in the A-6 community.

The upcoming A-6, with new engines, new wing, updated avionics and weapons systems, and additional wing stations for air-to-air and other ordnance, as well as command ejection, will greatly enhance the projection of naval air power. The Intruder is reputedly one of the few free-world aircraft that the USSR and her allies fear. Obviously the A-6 is and will be the backbone of naval striking power for some time to come.

David M. Stahlhut
CDR-USNR

A-6 WALK-AROUND

NOSE DETAILS

Beginning with this nose-on shot, and continuing through page 15, this series of photographs takes a "walk-around" look at the features of the basic A-6 aircraft. Features only on specific versions will usually be covered in the section covering that particular version. This head-on shot shows the shape of the intakes, the stance on the landing gear, and the angle of the wing fold.

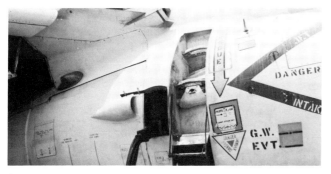

A number of details are visible in this shot of the right intake. The probe just forward of the top of the rescue arrow is the angle of attack sensor. The smaller probe in the jet intake chevron, just above the **D** in **DANGER** is the outside temperature probe. Within the open steps, just under the middle step, is the switch for opening and closing the canopy. The ground electrical connection is just aft of the steps, and the power cable is attached.

Under the right intake is the single point ground refueling point, and ahead of it, the little white spool is the Radar Beacon antenna which is part of the carrier landing system.

The in-flight refueling probe, radome, windscreen, canopy, and fixed intake ramp are seen here.

The left steps are seen here in the open position. Note the change to the low visibility markings on this aircraft.

This close-up of the left intake shows several more details. The intake cover is tied to the Total Temperature Probe. The static port is just ahead of the rescue arrow, and is outlined with a circle. There is also a canopy switch inside the left boarding steps, and the engine bay cooling scoop is also visible.

ON TOP

Above left: The inside of the canopy rails are seen in this view of a canopy that has been removed from the aircraft. The inside of the rails are flat black.

Above right: With the canopy removed, the area behind the seats is more visible than usual. There is a lot of plumbing and wiring located here.

Left: This view from the left side shows the continuation of the plumbing just under the skin on the spine of the aircraft.

Below left: This right side view shows more of the inner details along the top of the fuselage.

Below right: The top of the fuselage is seen here with all panels in place. The small scoop in the foreground is to supply positive pressure in the upper compartments of the aircraft, and the larger scoop was added with the TRAM modification to air-condition the aft avionics bay.

UNDERSIDE DETAILS

Above left and right: These two views show different angles of the undersides of the fuselage on an A-6E TRAM. Various scoops, slots, antennas and lights are visible. An external fuel tank is on the centerline station. The single point refueling receptacle is visible in the photo at left. The large circular hole under each engine is the DSC exhaust.

Just ahead of the tail hook is the chaff/flare dispenser. It is often covered with metal plates. For those who like the specific designations, this is the MX-7721/ALE-29A Dispenser Housing.

This view shows the centerline station with a buddy refueling store attached.

The fairing with **DO NOT PAINT** stenciled on the side is the Doppler Radar Antenna Fairing. The blade antenna is the UHF antenna. Note that the chaff/flare dispenser is covered with the plates in this photo.

The centerline station is seen from behind and to the right in this photo. Noteworthy is the different location for the UHF antenna on this aircraft. It is closer to the engine than the antenna seen in the photo at left. Both aircraft are A-6E TRAMs. It should be noted that during our research, we observed several examples where antennas and beacons were in different places on aircraft of the same type. Some had one lower beacon light, and others had two.

FUSELAGE DETAILS

The air-conditioning intake is at the leading edge of the right wing root as seen at left. The exhaust is just below the wing and ahead of the gear well. At right, part of the air-conditioning system is visible with the access panel removed.

A-6s had small fuselage lights on each side just above the engine, as seen in the photo at left. These have been replaced with formation light panels, as seen at right. There is no panel on the nose or tail, however, as is the case with most other aircraft. A panel has been added to the wing tips as seen on page 23.

The right formation light panel is seen just ahead of the word NAVY on this A-6E TRAM.

Originally the A-6 had speed brakes on either side of the fuselage, but these were found to be undesirable. They were originally perforated, as seen in the photo at center right, and they were bolted in the closed position so that they could not be used. Later, a solid plate was placed over the speed brake position as seen in this photo, and the hinges were also covered over.

TAIL & TAIL HOOK

Right and left side views of the tail section show the RHAW antenna fairing, tail beacon light, pitot probe, rudder, and the all-flying horizontal tail. Note that in the photo at right, the moving portion of the rudder also includes the tail fairing at the aft end of the fuselage. A small position light is on this fairing.

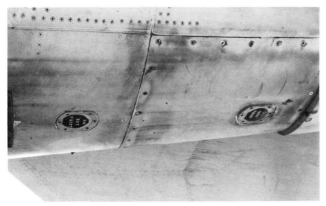 

Radar altimeter antennas are located under the tail section.

The fuel dump mast for the fuselage tanks is under the rudder fairing. Just ahead of it is the aft tie down point.

At left the tail hook is shown stowed in its cavity beneath the tail section. At right, the tail hook is seen in the lowered position.

NOSE LANDING GEAR DETAIL

These two photos show the nose landing gear used on the A-6A, A-6E, and KA-6D. Note the landing and taxi light at the center of the forward nose gear door and the lower beacon light on the right side of the door (left in the photo). The three approach lights are also visible.

This right side view shows that the oleo portion of the strut is at the top, and the torque link is visible. The side profile of the lower beacon light is visible.

As viewed from the left, the brace extending rearward into the wheel well is visible. This brace takes most of the load during a catapult launch.

With the addition of the turret on the A-6E TRAM, the lower beacon light was removed from the forward nose gear door, and relocated under the intake as seen in the photo at left. Although the turret is not installed on the aircraft at left, the flush plate that covers the turret location is visible. Turrets are not always present on TRAM aircraft. In the photo at right, the turret is present, and the need to relocate the beacon is evident. Note also that the small blade antenna, seen in the photos above, is no longer present in these photos.

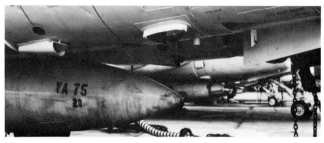

The relocated lower beacon on A-6E TRAMs is shown here. Another beacon is located in the same position under the left intake.

Above: The catapult launch arm fits into the catapult for launching. As demonstrated here, it takes little pressure to push the bar down.

Right: Nose gear well looking up and to the rear from the right.

Below: Right side of the nose gear well looking upward from under the left side door. Note the arm that opens and closes the door.

Nose gear well looking up and aft from the front right.

RIGHT MAIN LANDING GEAR

Right main landing gear showing the design of the wheel to good effect.

This inside view of the right main landing gear shows the strut, inside of the wheel, brake lines, and oleo details.

Right main gear as viewed from behind. Note the position of the doors.

This view is looking up and aft into the right main gear well. Note the arrangement of the forward doors in the foreground.

LEFT MAIN LANDING GEAR

Left main gear as seen from the inside with the aircraft up on jacks. This is the oleo extension that would be seen in an in-flight configuration with the gear extended.

Left main gear as seen from the front.

This view is looking straight up at the forward main gear doors. Note also the various lines along the side of the forward portion of the gear well.

Left main landing gear well.

ENGINE & ENGINE BAYS

The A-6 is powered by two J52P-8A engines that produce a combined 17,400 pounds of thrust. This view is looking down the left intake to the engine.

The left engine bay is seen opened up in this photo. The door is hinged at the top, and a single brace at the forward end holds the door open.

The right engine is seen here with the doors completely removed.

This is the right engine bay as viewed from the front showing the angle of the door and some of the details on the inside of the door.

Right engine exhaust as seen from behind.

The lower aft panel has been removed from below the tail pipe of the left engine. The curve of the tail pipe is visible in this view.

The J52P-8A turbojet is shown on a stand in front of the Intruder from which it was taken. The tail pipe has been removed.

What do you do with an engine when you have removed it from the aircraft for maintenance? In the case of the Intruder, you simply hang it on one of the pylons! This view shows the right side details.

In these two views the entire engine and the tail pipe are suspended from a pylon under the left wing. The bend in the tail pipe is clearly visible.

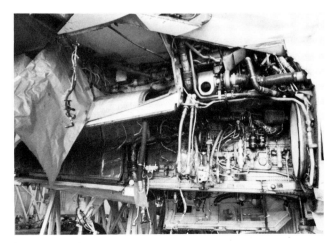

These two views show the right side engine bay with the engine removed.

WING DETAILS

WING FOLD, BRACE, & RAT

Above left and right: Wing fold details on the right and left wings are shown in these two photographs. Because of the location of the fold, the wing span is more than cut in half with the wings folded.

Left: Wing fold hinge on the left wing as viewed from above.

Below left: A brace is placed between the wing root and the folded part of each wing when the wings are folded.

Below right: The RAT is shown extended in this photo which was taken from behind.

As viewed from the front, the RAT is seen in the open position.

WING TIP DETAIL

Left: The left wing tip detail is seen from above. Note the boundary layer fence located just outside the national insignia and the fairings for the speed brake hinges.

Center left and right: The wing tips in these two views show the original light configuration. A green position light is located on the leading edge of the tip on the right wing, and a red light is on the left wing. There are no formation light panels.

The addition of formation light panels is visible on these two wing tips. The fairings, visible in all four photographs, house part of the radar homing and warning (RHAW) system.

LEADING EDGE SLATS

Above left and right: Leading edge slats on both wings are visible in these photos.

Left: This view shows the leading edge slat on the right wing.

Below left and right: With the slats removed, the area under the slats is visible here. This area is usually painted red regardless of the paint scheme on the aircraft.

FLAPS & SPOILERS

This is the left flap in the extended position as viewed from behind. Note the flap tracks on the outside of the flaps. The darker area is painted red. The small cutout just below the **500** is to provide clearance above a 300 gallon fuel tank when carried on the inboard pylon.

The left wing flap is shown here as viewed from under the wing tip. Flap guides are visible.

The spoilers on top of each wing are shown in these two photos. The spoilers are in two sections, being split at the wing fold.

Fully extended flaps are seen in these two views taken from above. Note the gap between the flap and the wing and spoiler. The clearance provided by the cutout above the fuel tanks is apparent here. Note how the flaps are split at the wing fold.

When the use of the fuselage speed brakes was discontinued, the wing tip speed brakes provided the in-flight braking for the Intruder. This view shows the right speed brake in the closed position.

This is the same view of the right speed brake as seen at left, but the brake is in the open position. Note the hinge fairings on the top and bottom portions of the brake.

WING TIP
SPEED BRAKES

Center left and right: The inside of open speed brakes are seen in these photos. The inside of the brakes are painted red. Fuel vents for jettisoning fuel from the wing tanks are located on the trailing edge just inboard of the speed brakes.

Left: Open speed brake as viewed from the outside. This view shows the angle of the fully open brakes.

PYLONS & EXTERNAL STORES

Four wing pylons and one centerline pylon carry the external stores on the A-6. These two views show the right inboard pylon. Note the open access panel door which is hinged at the top. This facilitates hooking up the various connections required by different stores. At left, the pylon is empty, and the anti-sway braces can be seen hanging down beneath the pylon. At right, a 300 gallon fuel tank is attached, and the door remains open. The anti-sway braces are tightened firmly down on top of the tank.

The left inboard pylon is seen here with a missile launch rail attached.

This inside view shows the outboard right pylon with a fuel tank attached.

An outside view reveals the outboard left pylon details with a fuel tank in place.

This close-up view shows the connections between the pylon and a MER.

EXTERNAL FUEL TANKS & BUDDY REFUELING STORES

External 300 gallon fuel tanks can be carried on all pylons. Those carried on wing pylons usually have a single vertical fin on the underside at the rear. Quite often the squadron color or emblem will be painted on this fin. These two photos show tanks on the outboard wing pylons. Note the angle of the tank to the pylon. The large low visibility gray insignia on the aircraft in the photo at left is both interesting and unusual.

An external fuel tank can also be carried on the fuselage station, but note that there is no fin at the aft end, and that the aft end is more rounded than on the tanks carried on the wing stations. This is to provide needed clearance between the tanks and the ground. Some centerline tanks have two fins. These fins are angled downward forty-five degrees from the horizontal centerline.

These two views show the buddy in-flight refueling store on the centerline station. Note that on the front end is a propeller that is turned by the airstream to generate power for the system. The drogue can be seen at the aft end of the store in the photo at right. It is reeled out on a hose behind the aircraft.

On this page and the next two, some of the ordnance usually carried by the A-6 is illustrated. However, it should be understood that this is by no means all of the ordnance carried by the Intruder. Many different stores can be carried by the aircraft, and space does not allow for all of them to be included. But most major stores are shown. Here a Laser Guided Bomb (LGB) is being loaded on the centerline pylon. Also noteworthy in this photo is the device attached to the leading edge of the outboard pylon. It looks something like the handle and stem on a canoe paddle, and is the ALQ-100 Radar Deception Antenna. Another similar antenna was carried on the left outboard pylon. This system has since been deleted from the Intruder. (U.S. Navy)

This MER has small practice bombs attached. It is on the right inboard pylon.

A Mk-83 2000 pound LGB is attached to the left outboard pylon. LGBs of the 1000, 2000, and 3000 pound classes can be carried by the Intruder.

These two photos show some of the other munitions certified for use on the A-6. In the photo at left, the two weapons in the foreground are aerial mines in bomb-like bodies with bomb fuses. They have the high drag fins on the aft end. The large cylinder is also an aerial mine. In the background is a MER with six 500 pound Mk-82 high drag bombs. In the photo at right, the three white cylinders are rocket launchers. The smaller one is for 2.75 inch rockets, and the larger two each carry four five inch rockets.

Above: Rockeye cluster bombs are loaded under the wing of this Intruder. Four weapons are on the MER on the outboard pylon, and two more are on a MER on the inboard pylon. The same arrangement would be repeated under the right wing for a total of twelve weapons.   (U.S. Navy)

Left: Another type of aerial mine is seen under the left inboard pylon.

Below: The Walleye guided glide bomb is also in the A-6 inventory of munitions. This is a training round. Noteworthy is the propeller at the aft end of the weapon which turns in the airstream to generate power. The small streamers were added to observe the air flow over the aft end of the weapon. These are not present on live Walleyes.
     (U.S. Navy)

MISSILES

The A-6 can carry the AIM-9 Sidewinder for air-to-air combat, but it takes up a pylon that could be used for air-to-ground weapons. Therefore the Sidewinder is seldom seen on an A-6.

One of the first missiles carried by the A-6 was the AGM-12 Bullpup shown here. Note that the missile is not mounted directly to the pylon, but to a launch rail that is attached under the pylon.

The AGM-53 Condor missile seemed to have great capabilities when tested, but it never entered the inventory.

The AGM-88A HARM (High-Velocity Anti-Radiation Missile) is seen under the left wing of an A-6E. It is used to attack enemy radars.

The AGM-84 Harpoon missile is one of the more formidable weapons carried by the A-6. This is a training version of the missile used to train ordnance personnel in ground handling and loading of the missile.

The AGM-65 Maverick is also carried by the A-6.

Another ARM carried by the A-6 is the AGM-78 Standard ARM. It was combat proven in Vietnam, and is seen here on the inboard left pylon.

EJECTION SEAT DETAIL

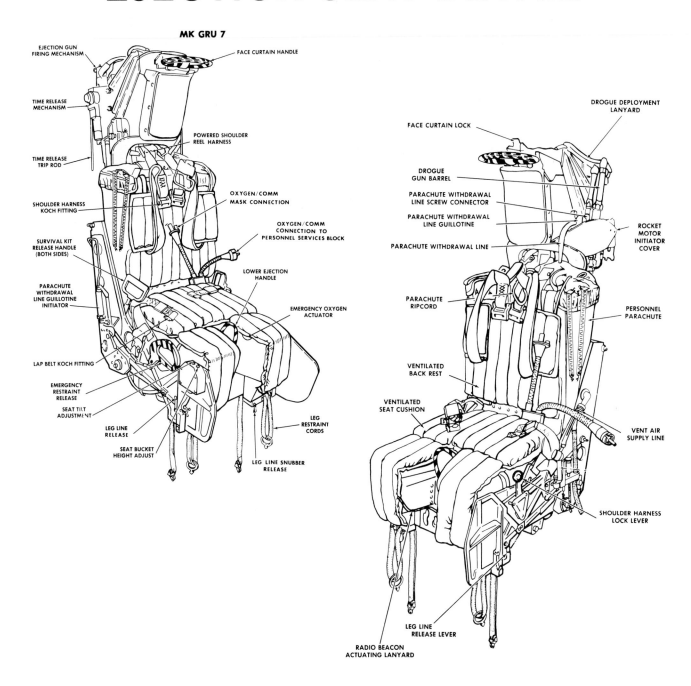

MK GRU 7

EJECTION GUN FIRING MECHANISM

FACE CURTAIN HANDLE

TIME RELEASE MECHANISM

POWERED SHOULDER REEL HARNESS

TIME RELEASE TRIP ROD

SHOULDER HARNESS KOCH FITTING

OXYGEN/COMM MASK CONNECTION

OXYGEN/COMM CONNECTION TO PERSONNEL SERVICES BLOCK

SURVIVAL KIT RELEASE HANDLE (BOTH SIDES)

LOWER EJECTION HANDLE

PARACHUTE WITHDRAWAL LINE GUILLOTINE INITIATOR

EMERGENCY OXYGEN ACTUATOR

LAP BELT KOCH FITTING

EMERGENCY RESTRAINT RELEASE

SEAT TILT ADJUSTMENT

LEG LINE RELEASE

SEAT BUCKET HEIGHT ADJUST

LEG LINE SNUBBER RELEASE

LEG RESTRAINT CORDS

DROGUE DEPLOYMENT LANYARD

FACE CURTAIN LOCK

DROGUE GUN BARREL

PARACHUTE WITHDRAWAL LINE SCREW CONNECTOR

PARACHUTE WITHDRAWAL LINE GUILLOTINE

PARACHUTE WITHDRAWAL LINE

ROCKET MOTOR INITIATOR COVER

PARACHUTE RIPCORD

PERSONNEL PARACHUTE

VENTILATED BACK REST

VENTILATED SEAT CUSHION

VENT AIR SUPPLY LINE

SHOULDER HARNESS LOCK LEVER

LEG LINE RELEASE LEVER

RADIO BEACON ACTUATING LANYARD

Details of the Martin Baker MK GRU 7 ejection seat are seen in this photo and the drawings above. Normal ejection is through the canopy. The reason for this is that if the canopy were jettisoned first, and were to stick in the open position, the crew would eject into the forward metal bracing of the canopy, and this would certainly prove fatal. Since the canopy is of the sliding type instead of the clamshell variety, there is not enough air flow under the canopy to ensure a clean separation in the event it hung up during the jettisoning process. Therefore, the seats and their occupants go right through the glass. This has caused some injuries in the past, to include those to LT Robert Goodman, but it is still considered desirable over the possibility of hitting the forward canopy brace.

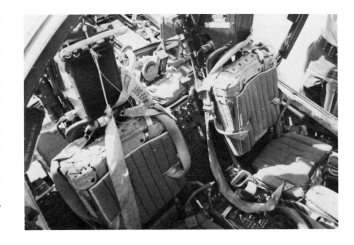

INTRUDER COLORS
ATLANTIC COAST NAVY SCHEMES

This is the CAG aircraft for VA-85 as photographed on February 2, 1978. *(Flightleader)*

Originally an A-6A, 155707 was remanufactured to A-6E standards, and is seen here in the markings of VA-34's **Blue Blasters** on October 20, 1977. *(Flightleader)*

VA-75 is represented by 158043, which was built as a production A-6E. The photograph is dated April 30, 1978. *(Flightleader)*

Another Atlantic coast squadron is VA-65 which is known as the **Tigers.** These were the squadron's markings in August 1975. *(Flightleader)*

An early A-6A (the 28th built) is shown here in overall chromate green. Surprisingly enough, aircraft are sometimes flown in this scheme prior to receiving their official paint scheme. *(Van Winkle)*

PACIFIC COAST NAVY SCHEMES

This beautiful in-flight shot shows the markings of VA-145's **Swordsmen.**   (U.S. Navy)

A-6A, 155600, is pictured on February 17, 1976, as the CAG aircraft from VA-196 aboard the USS Enterprise.

(Berganini via Leader)

VA-115 is represented by A-6A, 155715, on March 10, 1976. The aircraft was assigned to the **USS Midway** and is home based at Atsugi, Japan.   (Flightleader)

Another CAG aircraft, this time belonging to VA-165, is shown here in December 1975.   (Curry via Leader)

Dating back to July 1972, this photo shows A-6A, 152604, of VA-128, at NAS Whidbey Island, California. Whidbey Island is the home base for Pacific coast A-6 squadrons.

(Munkasy)

SUBDUED NAVY SCHEMES

As with other Navy aircraft, the A-6 has undergone a transition from colorful markings to the very subdued and colorless tactical schemes now in vogue. Unlike the F-14, for example, there was not a transition from the gray over white scheme to the overall gray scheme and then to the tactical scheme. The overall gray scheme was used very seldom on the A-6, and it is relatively difficult to find many photos of A-6s in that scheme. These two photos show two A-6s still in the gray over white scheme, but with colorless gray markings. It is interesting to note that in the photo at right, the national insignia on the fuselage is the small subdued gray type, while the large red, white, and blue insignia remains on both wings. In the photo at left, the gray insignia is used in all four positions. Both photos were taken on the same day in May 1984. The aircraft on the left belongs to VA-42, and the one on the right is assigned to VA-176.

These two photos were taken on the same day as the two photos above, and the same squadrons are represented, with VA-42 on the left and VA-176 on the right. Note the differences in the gray and blue-gray colors of the markings. Both aircraft are painted in two tones of the tactical blue-gray colors, but the demarcation between the two colors may be difficult to discern. VA-85's A-6s were painted in only one of the two colors on any given aircraft, but both colors were used. It was necessary to check the BuNo. of the aircraft to see which color it was supposed to be painted. The colors are so similar that it was impossible to tell the difference between two VA-85 aircraft parked next to each other that were painted in different colors.

VA-65's **Tigers** are represented again, this time by 155589. The aircraft is in only one color except for the radome which has two colors. It was impossible to find two A-6s in exactly the same markings on the day these five photographs were taken, even though every squadron except VA-34 was ashore.

A-6E TRAM COCKPIT

The pilot's instrument panel on an A-6E TRAM is shown here.

Left console detail.

The B/N's panel is shown here, and the scope has the hood in place.

Center console detail. Keys to the A-6E TRAM cockpit are on page 55.

View looking down into the B/N's position. The right console and center radar control console are visible.

KA-6D COCKPIT

This KA-6D was tanking from a KC-130 as this photo was taken. The lack of all of the B/N's equipment is evident in this photo.   *(U.S. Navy)*

These two photos show the instrument panel in a KA-6D. Note the lack of instruments on the right side, and the placard indicating G-limit restrictions for the aircraft. The KA-6D is G-limited to extend airframe life.

Left and center consoles in a KA-6D.

Center and right console detail. Only one panel on the right console has any switches. Keys for the KA-6D cockpit are on page 60.

KA-6D COLORS

KA-6D tanker aircraft are assigned to the attack squadrons, and wear the same colors as their bomber counterparts. Often, but by no means always, they have a band around the aft fuselage to easily signify them as a tanker in the air. This band was in the squadron color in the days of colorful schemes, and in a light gray or blue-gray in the tactical schemes. However, it should be noted that tankers did not transition to the tactical scheme as fast as the bombers, and carried colorful markings well into 1985 in some cases. This tanker belongs to VA-196, and was photographed in May 1981.   (Grove via Leader)

A diagonal fuselage band is on this KA-6D from VA-176. The photo was taken on April 28, 1979.   (Flightleader)

October 20, 1977, is the date on this photo of KA-6D, 152611, from VA-65.   (Flightleader)

The only color on this VA-75 tanker is the fuselage band, national insignia, and some of the smaller detail markings. Tail markings have gone to the subdued black variety.
(Grove via Leader)

Almost all of the markings on the KA-6D are in the low visibility gray. The aircraft remains in the gray over white scheme, but there is no fuselage band.   (Van Winkle)

MARINE INTRUDERS

An all-blue tail with a white hawk indicates that this A-6A belongs to VMA-AW-533. Blue and white checkerboards are on the rudder and fin of the fuel tank. The photo is dated June 12, 1981. *(Van Winkle)*

Markings for VMAT-AW-202 include an all-red tail and a KC tail code. When photographed, this A-6A Intruder was on a stopover at El Paso International Airport in March 1977.

The **Green Knights** of VMA-AW-121 operated this A-6E which was photographed in September 1979, at Holloman AFB, New Mexico.

Another Marine unit that formerly had an all-white tail was VMA-AW-224. This time the tail markings are in red. The aircraft is A-6E, 159316, and it was photographed on October 29, 1977. *(Flightleader)*

The **Polka Dots** of VMA-AW-332 formerly had a dark blue vertical tail with an orange and yellow moon, but the change to more subdued markings is seen in this photo taken on September 25, 1981. While color remains in the national insignia and the smaller standard markings, unit markings are now all white. This indicates a move toward the low visibility markings for Marine Intruders.

(Van Winkle)

While still in the gray over white scheme, this Marine KA-6D shows more indication of the move to low visibility markings. In this case, markings, to include the national insignia, are a medium gray. The photo is dated September 1983.

(Grove via Leader)

UNDER THE RADOME

Above left: The radome on Intruders hinges at the top and opens like this to allow maintenance. It still takes a pretty tall man or a good stool to reach the radar and other components inside. Note that some of the equipment hinges out to the side on a pallet, providing easier access.

Above right: This head-on photo shows the radar and some of the associated equipment under the radome. The aircraft is an A-6E TRAM.

Left: Close-up view of the radar antenna dish on an A-6E TRAM.

Below left and right: There is no radar in the KA-6D as evidenced in these two views. Instead, various electronic gear is mounted on two shelves. The green spheres carry oxygen.

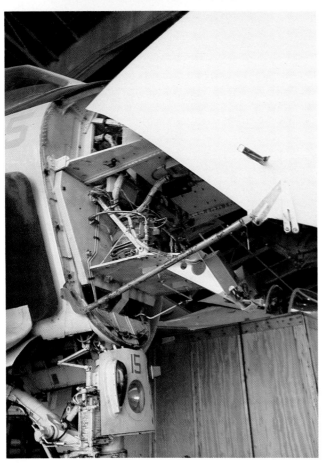

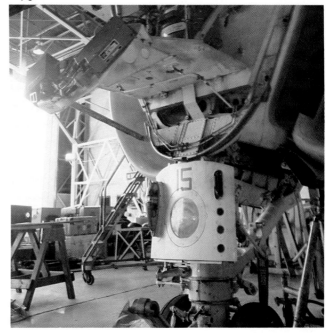

DIMENSIONS

DIMENSION	ACTUAL	1/100th SCALE	1/72nd SCALE	1/48th SCALE
Length (Normal)	54' 9 "	6.57"	9.13"	13.68"
Wing Span (Extended)	53' 0 "	6.36"	8.83"	13.25"
Wing Span (Folded)	25' 4 "	3.04"	4.22"	6.33"
Height (To top of tail)	16' 2 "	1.94"	2.69"	4.04"
Height (With wings folding)	21' 11"	2.63"	3.65"	5.48"
Height (To tips of wings)	7' 10"	.94"	1.31"	1.96"
Height (To top of canopy)	12' 5 "	1.49"	2.07"	3.10"
Height (To TRAM turret)	3' 9 "	.45"	.63"	.94"
Height (To pylons)	6' 3 "	.75"	1.04"	1.56"
Tail Span	20' 5 "	2.45"	3.40"	5.10"
Wheel Track	17' 2 "	2.06"	2.86"	4.29"
Wheel Tread	11' 0 "	1.32"	1.83"	2.75"

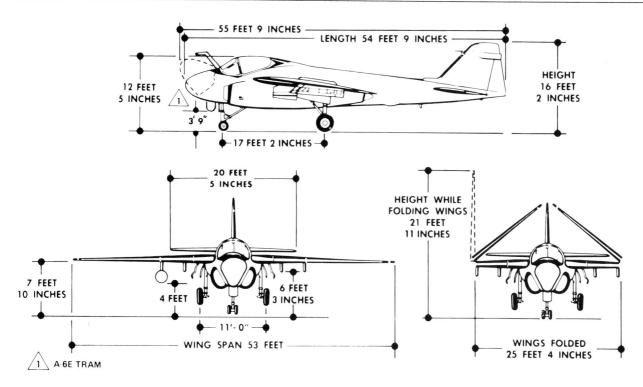

A-6E TRAM DATA

Empty Weight	26,320 lbs.
Internal Fuel	15,940 lbs.
Max External Stores	18,000 lbs.
Max Speed	563 knots
Cruise Speed	415 knots
Approach Speed	111 knots
Field T.O. Distance	1790 feet
Field Landing Distance	1860 feet
Service Ceiling	47,200 feet
Ferry Range	2378 N.M.

This nose-on view of an A-6E shows the relative compactness of the rather large Intruder when the wings are folded. The aircraft is from VA-115 assigned to the USS Midway, and the photo was taken on May 30, 1981. (Cockle)

1/72nd SCALE FIVE-VIEW DRAWINGS

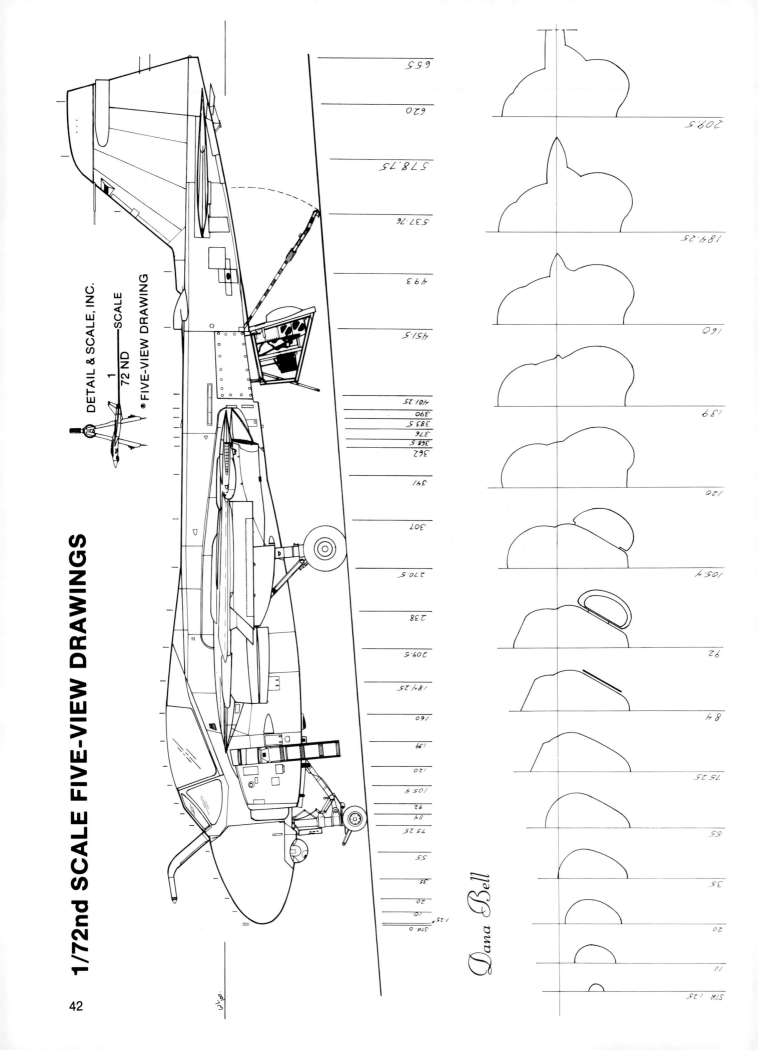

DETAIL & SCALE, INC.

1
72 ND   SCALE

● FIVE-VIEW DRAWING

Dana Bell

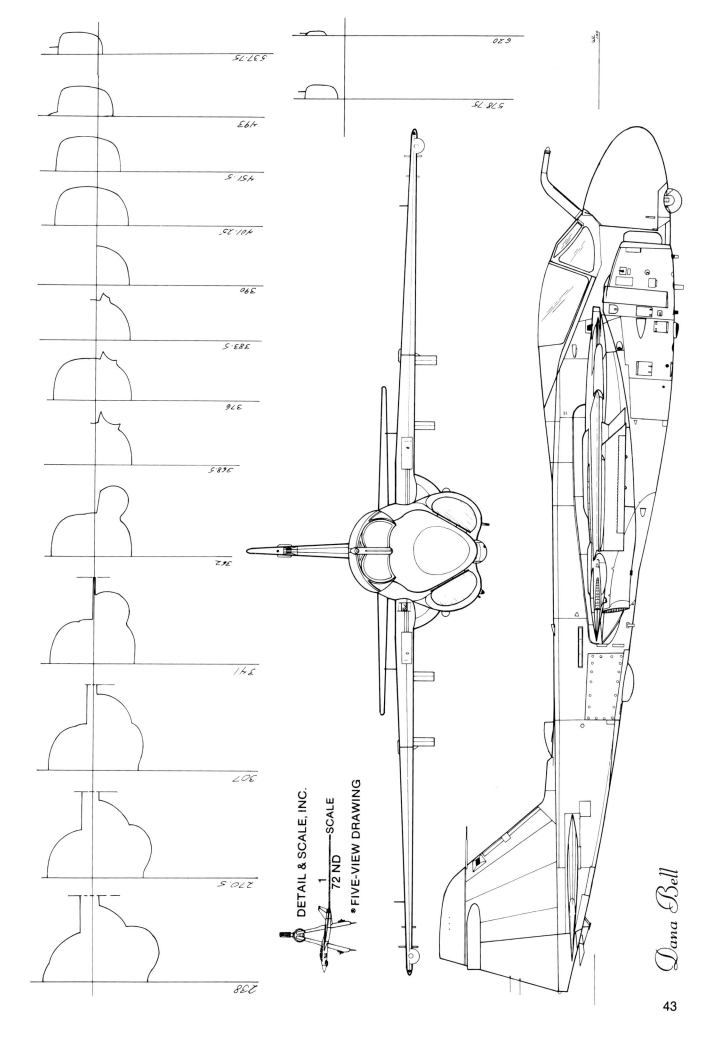

DETAIL & SCALE, INC.

1
72 ND SCALE

★FIVE-VIEW DRAWING

Dana Bell

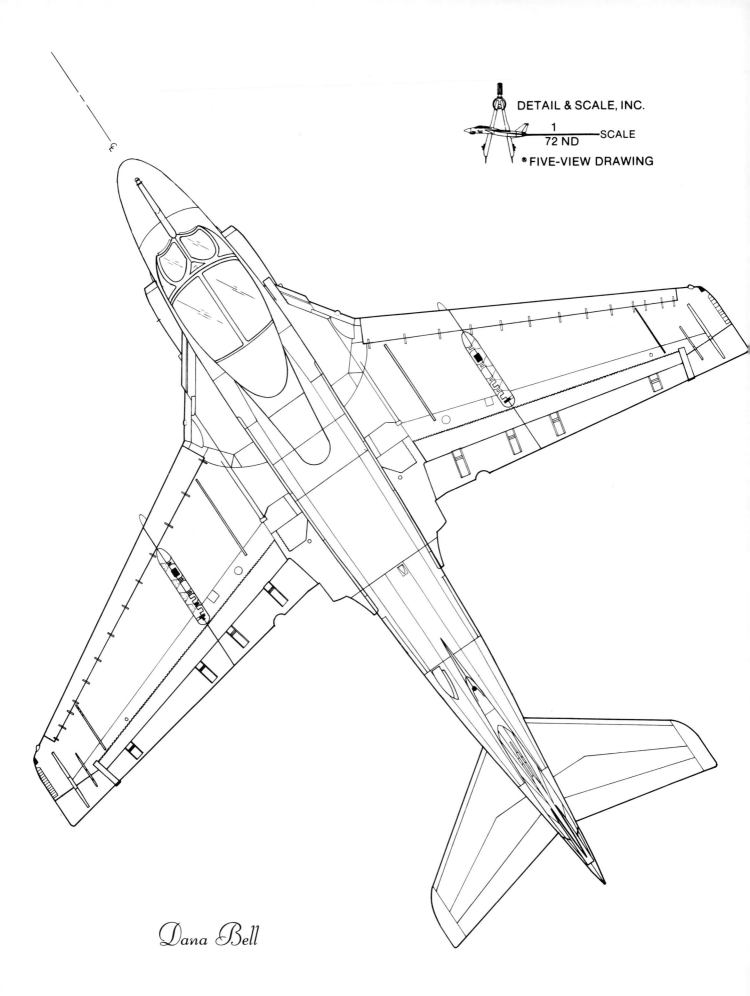

DETAIL & SCALE, INC.

$\frac{1}{72 \text{ ND}}$ ──── SCALE

® FIVE-VIEW DRAWING

Dana Bell

Dana Bell

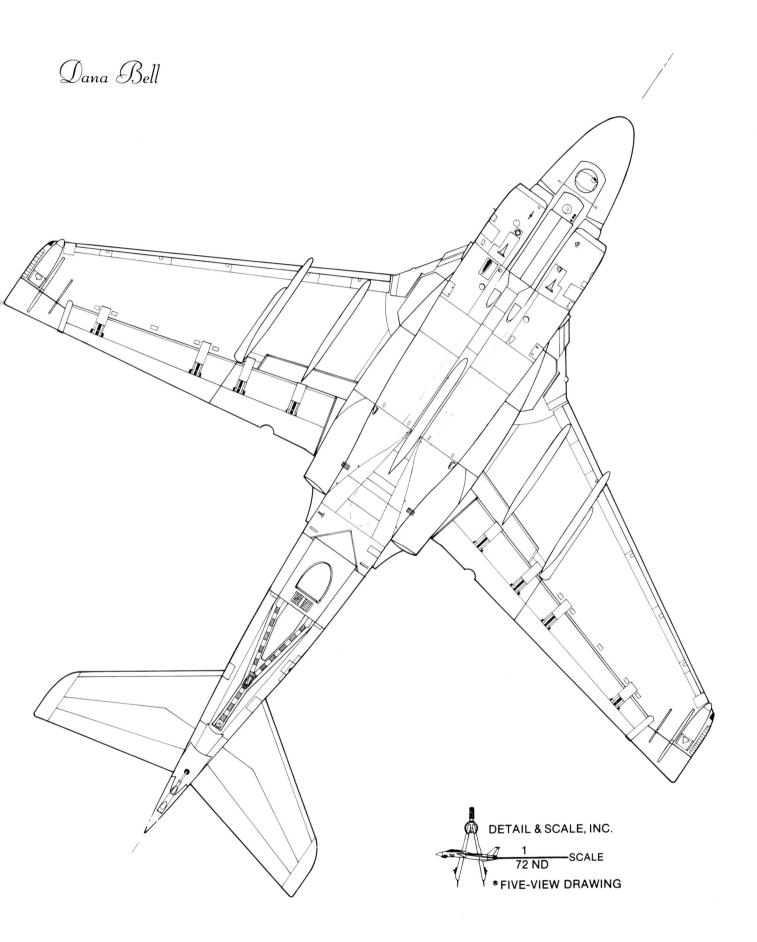

DETAIL & SCALE, INC.

$\dfrac{1}{72\text{ ND}}$ SCALE

® FIVE-VIEW DRAWING

A-6A

*The A-6A was the first production attack version of the Intruder produced. A-6A, 155662, of the **Green Pawns**, VA-42, is seen here in June 1974. VA-42 is the RAG unit for the Atlantic Coast Intruder squadrons.* *(Geer)*

The A-6A was the first production version of the Intruder, and a total of 488 were produced. By the time the A-6A entered service in March 1963, with the Atlantic coast RAG squadron, VA-42, all major airframe changes that were to be made to the Intruder had already been made. The only further visible changes of any consequence would be the addition of the TRAM turret and additional air scoop and exhaust for aft electronics bay cooling with the A-6E TRAM. Further changes will undoubtedly take place with the A-6F, but these are yet to be finalized.

After VA-42, the first operational squadron was VA-75 in 1964. It was VA-75, known as the "Sunday Punchers," that took the Intruder into combat over Vietnam on July 1, 1965, aboard the USS INDEPENDENCE. VA-85's "Black Falcons" followed VA-75, flying from the USS KITTY HAWK. Other squadrons followed, and while Atlantic coast squadrons deployed to the Pacific and Vietnam, they temporarily wore tail codes beginning with the letter N instead of their usual A. The Marines also took the A-6A to Vietnam, and like the Navy, met with considerable success. Thus the A-6A became the only combat proven attack version of the Intruder in the skies over Vietnam. There were lessons learned, and improvements were made, but the all-weather bombing capability of the aircraft had proven out, and reports indicated that it was better than expected. However, the maintenance time required on the sophisticated systems in the Intruder caused a relatively low in-service rate, and a high number of man hours to flight hours. This has been improved over the years and with the newer models, but it only follows that the more sophisticated an aircraft is, the more work it takes to keep it fully operational.

The A-6A had an empty weight of 26,350 pounds, and a maximum take-off weight of 60,625 pounds. A total of 18,000 pounds of payload could be carried including fuel

and ordnance. From shore bases it had a take-off roll of 1,940 feet, and could land in 1,860 feet. It had a maximum speed of 625 miles per hour, and a service ceiling of 47,200 feet. Its ferry range was a little over 3,000 nautical miles. A proposed three-seat TA-6A training version was never built.

As improvements in state-of-the-art avionics and weapons delivery systems paved the way for the second generation A-6E, many of the A-6A airframes were converted to other versions. Some became KA-6D tankers, others were used in the A-6B and A-6C programs, but the largest number were converted to A-6Es, and remain in service in the TRAM configuration today. Any A-6E TRAM seen today with a BuNo. of 157029 or earlier was originally an A-6A. Production A-6E airframes began with 158041. A listing of A-6A production, to include the early test and evaluation aircraft, by fiscal year is as follows:

Year	BuNos	Total
1959	147864-147867	4
1960	148615-148618	4
1961	149475-149486	12
1962	149935-149958	24
1963	151558-151600	43
1964	151780-151827	48
1965	152583-152646	64
1966	152891-152923	33
1967 (1)	152924-152954	31
1967 (2)	154124-154171	48
1968	155644-155725	82
1969	156998-157029	32
	TOTAL BUILT	488

A-6A GENERAL ARRANGEMENT

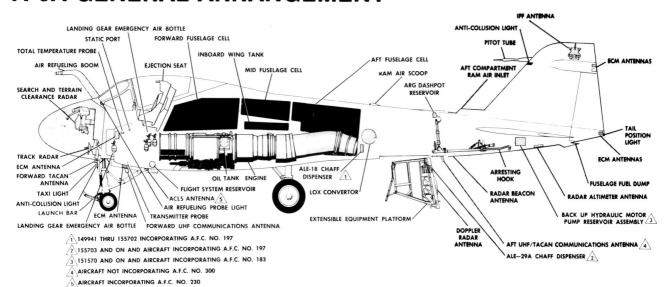

LANDING GEAR EMERGENCY AIR BOTTLE
STATIC PORT
FORWARD FUSELAGE CELL
TOTAL TEMPERATURE PROBE
AIR REFUELING BOOM
INBOARD WING TANK
MID FUSELAGE CELL
EJECTION SEAT
SEARCH AND TERRAIN CLEARANCE RADAR
AFT FUSELAGE CELL
KAM AIR SCOOP
ARG DASHPOT RESERVOIR
IFF ANTENNA
ANTI-COLLISION LIGHT
PITOT TUBE
AFT COMPARTMENT RAM AIR INLET
ECM ANTENNAS
TRACK RADAR
ECM ANTENNA
FORWARD TACAN ANTENNA
TAXI LIGHT
ANTI-COLLISION LIGHT
LAUNCH BAR
ECM ANTENNA
LANDING GEAR EMERGENCY AIR BOTTLE
OIL TANK ENGINE
FLIGHT SYSTEM RESERVOIR
ACLS ANTENNA /5\
AIR REFUELING PROBE LIGHT
TRANSMITTER PROBE
FORWARD UHF COMMUNICATIONS ANTENNA
ALE-18 CHAFF DISPENSER /1\
LOX CONVERTOR
EXTENSIBLE EQUIPMENT PLATFORM
DOPPLER RADAR ANTENNA
ARRESTING HOOK
RADAR BEACON ANTENNA
TAIL POSITION LIGHT
ECM ANTENNAS
FUSELAGE FUEL DUMP
RADAR ALTIMETER ANTENNA
BACK UP HYDRAULIC MOTOR PUMP RESERVOIR ASSEMBLY /3\
AFT UHF/TACAN COMMUNICATIONS ANTENNA /4\
ALE-29A CHAFF DISPENSER /2\

/1\ 149941 THRU 155702 INCORPORATING A.F.C. NO. 197
/2\ 155703 AND ON AND AIRCRAFT INCORPORATING A.F.C. NO. 197
/3\ 151570 AND ON AND AIRCRAFT INCORPORATING A.F.C. NO. 183
/4\ AIRCRAFT NOT INCORPORATING A.F.C. NO. 300
/5\ AIRCRAFT INCORPORATING A.F.C. NO. 230

The A-6A saw extensive service in Vietnam. Here A-6A, 151782, is seen returning to the USS KITTY HAWK after a mission. Mission markers are painted on the intake. VA-85 is an Atlantic coast unit, but during this Vietnam tour, it carried the Pacific coast tail code of NH. (Paul via Geer)

The Marines also operated the A-6A, as evidenced by this May 1974 photo of 157005. This was one of the last batch of A-6As built. (Geer)

This photo shows another VA-85 A-6A, again assigned to a Pacific coast carrier for duty in Vietnam. This time the carrier is the USS CONSTELLATION, and the tail code is NK. The photo was taken at NAS North Island in October 1969. (Kasulka via Geer)

This photo shows the cockpit details of the A-6A. Keys for the cockpit details are on the following page.

(Grumman)

A-6A COCKPIT LAYOUT

PILOT'S STATION

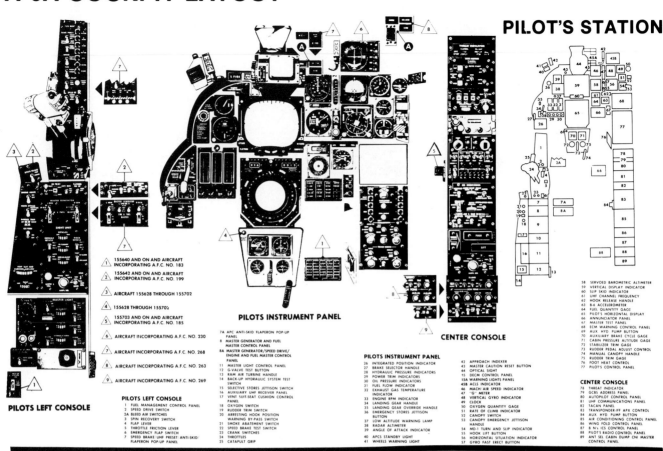

PILOTS INSTRUMENT PANEL

1. 155640 AND ON AND AIRCRAFT INCORPORATING A.F.C. NO. 183
2. 155642 AND ON AND AIRCRAFT INCORPORATING A.F.C. NO. 199
3. AIRCRAFT 155628 THROUGH 155702
4. 155628 THROUGH 155702
5. 155703 AND ON AND AIRCRAFT INCORPORATING A.F.C. NO. 185
6. AIRCRAFT INCORPORATING A.F.C. NO. 230
7. AIRCRAFT INCORPORATING A.F.C. NO. 268
8. AIRCRAFT INCORPORATING A.F.C. NO. 263
9. AIRCRAFT INCORPORATING A.F.C. NO. 269

PILOTS LEFT CONSOLE

1. FUEL MANAGEMENT CONTROL PANEL
2. SPEED DRIVE SWITCH
2A. BLEED AIR SWITCHES
3. SPIN RECOVERY SWITCH
4. FLAP LEVER
5. THROTTLE FRICTION LEVER
6. EMERGENCY FLAP SWITCH
7. SPEED BRAKE/UHF PRESET/ANTI-SKID/FLAPERON POP-UP PANEL

7A. APC ANTI-SKID FLAPERON POP-UP PANEL
8. MASTER GENERATOR AND FUEL MASTER CONTROL PANEL
8A. MASTER GENERATOR/SPEED DRIVE/ENGINE AND FUEL MASTER CONTROL PANEL
11. MASTER LIGHT CONTROL PANEL
12. G-VALVE TEST BUTTON
13. HYDRAULIC PRESSURE INDICATORS
14. RAM AIR TURBINE HANDLE
15. BACK-UP HYDRAULIC SYSTEM TEST SWITCH
16. SELECTIVE STORES JETTISON SWITCH
17. VENT SUIT-SEAT CUSHION CONTROL PANEL
18. OXYGEN SWITCH
19. RUDDER TRIM SWITCH
20. ARRESTING HOOK POSITION WARNING BY-PASS SWITCH
21. SMOKE ABATEMENT SWITCH
22. SPEED BRAKE TEST SWITCH
23. CRANK SWITCHES
24. THROTTLES
25. CATAPULT GRIP

PILOTS INSTRUMENT PANEL

26. INTEGRATED POSITION INDICATOR
27. BRAKE SELECTOR HANDLE
28. HYDRAULIC PRESSURE INDICATORS
29. POWER TRIM INDICATORS
30. OIL PRESSURE INDICATORS
31. FUEL FLOW INDICATOR
32. EXHAUST GAS TEMPERATURE INDICATOR
33. ENGINE RPM INDICATOR
34. LANDING GEAR HANDLE
35. LANDING GEAR OVERRIDE HANDLE
36. EMERGENCY STORES JETTISON BUTTON
37. LOW ALTITUDE WARNING LAMP
38. RADAR ALTIMETER
39. ANGLE OF ATTACK INDICATOR
40. APCS STANDBY LIGHT
41. WHEELS WARNING LIGHT

42. APPROACH INDEXER
43. MASTER CAUTION RESET BUTTON
44. OPTICAL SIGHT
45. DECM CONTROL PANEL
45A. WARNING LIGHTS PANEL
45B. ACLS INDICATOR
46. MACH/AIR SPEED INDICATOR
47. "G" METER
48. VERTICAL GYRO INDICATOR
49. CLOCK
50. OXYGEN QUANTITY GAGE
51. RATE OF CLIMB INDICATOR
52. CANOPY SWITCH
53. CANOPY EMERGENCY JETTISON HANDLE
54. MD-1 TURN AND SLIP INDICATOR
55. HOOK LIFT BUTTON
56. HORIZONTAL SITUATION INDICATOR
57. GYRO FAST ERECT BUTTON

58. SERVOED BAROMETRIC ALTIMETER
59. VERTICAL DISPLAY INDICATOR
60. SLIP SKID INDICATOR
61. UHF CHANNEL FREQUENCY
62. HOOK RELEASE HANDLE
63. 8-A ACCELEROMETER
64. FUEL QUANTITY GAGE
65. PILOT'S HORIZONTAL DISPLAY
66. ANNUNCIATOR PANEL
67. MASTER TEST PANEL
68. ECM WARNING CONTROL PANEL
69. AUX HYD PUMP BUTTON
70. AUXILIARY BRAKE CYCLE GAGE
71. CABIN PRESSURE ALTITUDE GAGE
72. STABILIZER TRIM GAGE
73. RUDDER PEDAL ADJUST CONTROL
74. MANUAL CANOPY HANDLE
75. RUDDER TRIM GAGE
76. FOOT HEAT CONTROL
77. PILOT'S CONTROL PANEL

CENTER CONSOLE

78. THREAT INDICATOR
79. GCBS ADDRESS PANEL
80. AUTOPILOT CONTROL PANEL
81. UHF COMMUNICATIONS PANEL
82. TACAN PANEL
83. TRANSPONDER-IFF APX CONTROL
84. AUX. HYD. PUMP BUTTON
85. AIR CONDITIONING CONTROL PANEL
86. WING FOLD CONTROL PANEL
87. B N's ICS CONTROL PANEL
88. PILOT'S RADIO CONTROL PANEL
89. ANT SEL CABIN DUMP CNI MASTER CONTROL PANEL

BOMBARDIER'S STATION

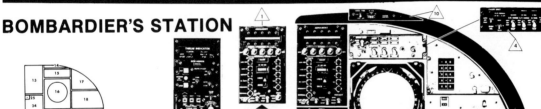

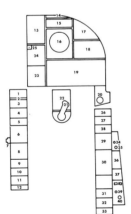

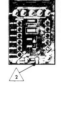

CENTER CONSOLE **BOMBARDIER/NAVIGATOR'S INSTRUMENT PANEL** **BOMBARDIER/NAVIGATOR'S RIGHT CONSOLE**

CENTER CONSOLE

1. THREAT INDICATOR
2. GCBS ADDRESS PANEL
3. AUTOPILOT CONTROL PANEL
4. UHF COMMUNICATIONS PANEL
5. TACAN PANEL
6. TRANSPONDER-IFF/APX CONTROL
7. AUX. HYD. PUMP BUTTON
8. AIR CONDITIONING CONTROL PANEL
9. WING FOLD CONTROL PANEL
10. B/N's ICS CONTROL PANEL
11. PILOT'S RADIO CONTROL PANEL
12. ANT SEL/CABIN DUMP/CNI MASTER CONTROL PANEL

BOMBARDIER/NAVIGATOR'S INSTRUMENT PANEL

13. ARMAMENT CONTROL PANEL
14. 1C-IR COOLING CONTROL PANEL
15. ECM CONTROL PANEL
16. DIRECT VIEW INDICATOR
17. ATTACK NAVIGATION PANEL
18. NAVIGATION CONTROL PANEL
19. BOMBARDIER/NAVIGATOR'S CONTROL PANEL
20. OUTSIDE AIR TEMPERATURE GAGE
21. BOMBARDIER/NAVIGATOR'S SLEW CONTROL
22. COMPUTER KEYBOARD
23. MODE SELECTOR PANEL
24. FUZING CONTROL PANEL
25. MASTER ARM SWITCH

BOMBARDIER/NAVIGATOR'S RIGHT CONSOLE

26. AUXILIARY ARMAMENT CONTROL PANEL
27. MULTIPLE RELEASE PANEL
28. SINS ICS AND PLATFORM INFLT ALIGN PANEL
29. DOPPLER PLATFORM CONTROL PANEL
30. ERECTION CONTROLLER PANEL
31. RADIO CONTROL PANEL

32. CHAFF DISPENSER CONTROL PANEL
33. GROUND CONTROL BOMBING SYSTEM CONTROL PANEL
34. OXYGEN SWITCH
35. MASTER TEST BUTTON
36. INTERIOR LIGHTING CONTROL PANEL
37. LB-31A CAMERA POD CONTROL PANEL
38. VENT SUIT-SEAT CUSHION CONTROL
39. BOMB TONE SWITCH
40. G-VALVE TEST BUTTON

1. 155642 AND ON AND AIRCRAFT INCORPORATING A.F.C. NO. 166
2. 155659 AND ON
3. 155703 AND ON AND AIRCRAFT INCORPORATING A.F.C. NO. 185
4. 155703 AND ON AND AIRCRAFT INCORPORATING A.F.C. NO. 197
5. AIRCRAFT INCORPORATING A.F.C. NO. 263
6. AIRCRAFT INCORPORATING A.F.C. NO. 230
7. 152937 THROUGH 157027 INCORPORATING A.F.C. NO. 256
8. AIRCRAFT INCORPORATING A.F.C. NO. 287
9. AIRCRAFT INCORPORATING A.F.C. NO. 269
10. AIRCRAFT INCORPORATING A.V.C. NO. 1433

AFT BULKHEAD CONSOLE

41. ACLS CONTROL PANEL
42. RADAR BEACON CONTROL PANEL
43. KY-28 CONTROL PANEL
44. MA-1 COMPASS CONTROL PANEL

AFT BULKHEAD CONSOLE

A-6B

Nineteen A-6Bs were converted from A-6A airframes to carry the Standard ARM. Three modifications were tried, each with varying degrees of sophistication. *(Grumman)*

The original A-6B proposal was for a clear air attack version of the Intruder with no all weather capability. However, this version was never built and the A-6B designator went to a program to develop an Intruder optimized for the air defense (or SAM) suppression mission. There were a total of nineteen A-6Bs built, and all were conversions of existing A-6A airframes. In actuality, there were three different modifications within the A-6B program. One was called Mod. O, another Mod. 1, and the third, PAT/ARM for Passive Angle Tracking/Anti-Radiation Missile. Ten aircraft received the Mod. O conversion, six the Mod. 1, and three the PAT/ARM conversion. All carried the AGM-78 Standard anti-radiation missile. Additionally, the usual ordnance certified for use with the A-6 could also be carried. These aircraft were placed in squadron service and served in Vietnam in the same role as the better known "Wild Weasels" of the Air Force. Later, these aircraft were reconfigured as A-6Es. It should be noted that the Standard ARM is carried by conventional A-6s as well.

This A-6B is shown on take off with two Standard ARMs. Note the small nodes on the radome. These were antennas intended to detect radar emissions. *(Grumman)*

Cockpit detail in one of the A-6B test aircraft. *(Grumman)*

Twelve A-6Cs were converted from A-6A airframes. This version of the Intruder carried special electro-optical sensors to detect targets that provided poor radar imagery. The large sensor is seen on the centerline of this aircraft. (Grumman)

A-6C

While the A-6A possessed an outstanding ability to detect and destroy targets in all types of weather by day or night, it relied on its radar for target detection. However, some targets simply are not detectable by radar. A case in point were the vehicles being used to bring supplies down trails and roads from the north in Vietnam. The North Vietnamese would use the cover of darkness to protect these vehicles from visual detection, and they did not show up on radar. To deal with this situation, the A-6C was developed, and like the A-6B, was converted from existing A-6A airframes as they came off the production lines. A total of twelve A-6Cs were built.

To detect these targets, the A-6C was fitted with a special sensor pod known as TRIM, which stood for Trails, Roads, Interdiction Multisensor. It was comprised of both FLIR (Forward-Looking Infrared), and LLL-TV (Low-Light-Level Television) systems. There is also a direction finder which indicates targets on a video display. These systems could detect vehicles, trains, and other targets in poor light and at night, thereby greatly increasing the night capability of the Intruder. However, it should be remembered that such electro-optical equipment does not work well in poor weather such as fog, clouds, and rain.

The pods were first evaluated in 1968 on one of the original airframes, BuNo. 147867, as seen on the next page. Two pods were carried under the wings on additional pylons fitted on the outboard or folding wing panels. However, a pod with a turret was eventually selected and carried on the centerline station as seen in the photograph above. The first use in combat was not until 1970, with VA-165, which operated from the USS AMERICA.

After Vietnam, almost all of the A-6Cs were converted to A-6Es. Today, the TRAM's multi-sensor provides detection of targets not easily detectable by radar.

Three photos above: Different sensors are visible under the wings of test aircraft number 4. The rather large and bulky sensors are mounted on an additional non-standard pylon outboard of the wing fold. (Grumman)

Left: Some sort of camera was mounted to the left of the windscreen on the aircraft shown above. This is a close-up of that camera fairing.

A-6E & A-6E TRAM

The A-6E and A-6E TRAM marked an improvement over the all-weather delivery capability of the A-6A. This A-6E TRAM belongs to VA-145.

(Cockle)

While the A-6A demonstrated outstanding qualities as an all-weather attack aircraft, its DIANE weapons delivery and navigation systems were based on technology from the mid-to-late 1950s. The advances in technology over the following decade provided much room for improving the system into an even better one. This resulted in the development of the second attack version of the Intruder which became the A-6E. Three major areas were addressed in the upgrade. First was the radar systems. The A-6A had an AN/APQ-92 search radar, and an AN/APQ-112 track radar. For the A-6E, these two radars were replaced by a single AN/APQ-148 multi-mode radar that combined both search and track functions as well as terrain avoidance. Handling one radar instead of two reduced crew workload.

The second major area of improvement was with the general purpose computer. In the A-6E, the AN/ASQ-133 solid state digital computer, manufactured by IBM, replaced the AN/ASQ-61 in the A-6A. This was a proven computer, already used in the EA-6B Prowler, the A-7, and the Air Force's F-111. The third area to be improved was the weapons release system. The new system featured solid-state circuitry and had an increased self-test capability. All of this not only went to improve the Intruder's capabilities, but also reportedly reduced the maintenance requirements in terms of man-hours to flight hours, and improved system reliability.

The prototype for the A-6E was a converted A-6A, BuNo. 155673, and it made its first flight on February 27, 1970. It was the first conversion of an A-6A to an A-6E, and

many more would follow -- so many in fact that well over one-half of the A-6Es produced were converted from existing A-6A airframes. A-6Es produced as new airframes began down the assembly line under the fiscal 1970 budget, the first carrying BuNo. 158041. Soon A-6Es began to enter service in Atlantic coast Navy squadrons. As with the A-6A, the first squadron to operate the A-6E was the Atlantic coast RAG squadron, VA-42, which received its first A-6Es in late 1971. VA-85 became the first operational squadron shortly thereafter, and was followed in succession by other Atlantic coast squadrons.

It was not until 1974 that the Pacific RAG squadron, VA-128, received its first A-6Es. It was also 1974 before the first Marine squadron, VMAT(AW)-202, received A-6Es at their home base of Cherry Point.

With the success of the TRIM equipment in the A-6C, the increased capabilities derived from electro-optical systems in detecting non-radar type targets resulted in a new system and a new acronym -- TRAM, which stands for Target Recognition and Attack Multisensor. For the first time in the Intruder's operational history, there was a clearly noticeable difference in the aircraft's physical appearance. A turret with the sensors located in it appeared beneath the radome just forward of the nose gear. However, this turret was far less noticeable than the large pod/turret combination carried by the A-6C, and it did not take up a pylon needed for fuel or ordnance. At first this turret did not appear on all A-6E TRAMs, because the equipment was not always ready

A-6E GENERAL ARRANGEMENT

Labels on diagram:

LANDING GEAR EMERGENCY AIR BOTTLE
STATIC PORT
TOTAL TEMPERATURE PROBE
AIR REFUELING BOOM
FORWARD FUSELAGE CELL
INBOARD WING TANK
MID FUSELAGE CELL
SEARCH AND TERRAIN CLEARANCE RADAR
EJECTION SEAT
AFT FUSELAGE CELL
RAM AIR SCOOP
ARG DASHPOT RESERVOIR 2
IFF ANTENNA 1
ANTI-COLLISION LIGHT
PITOT TUBE
UHF/IFF ANTENNA 2
ECM ANTENNAS
AFT COMPARTMENT RAM AIR INLET
TAIL POSITION LIGHT
ECM ANTENNAS
ACLS RECEIVER AND ANTENNA 2 4
DRS TURRET 2
ECM ANTENNA 1
FORWARD TACAN ANTENNA
TAXI LIGHT
ANTICOLLISION LIGHT 1
LAUNCH BAR
ECM ANTENNA
LANDING GEAR EMERGENCY AIR BOTTLE
OIL TANK ENGINE
ANTICOLLISION LIGHT 2
FLIGHT SYSTEMS RESERVOIR 2
TACAN ANTENNA 2
AIR REFUELING PROBE LIGHT
TRANSMITTER PROBE
FORWARD UHF COMMUNICATIONS ANTENNA 1
ACLS ANTENNA 2 4
LOX CONVERTOR
VIDEO RECORDER
EXTENSIBLE EQUIPMENT PLATFORM
ARRESTING HOOK
RADAR BEACON ANTENNA
DOPPLER RADAR ANTENNA
AFT UHF/TACAN COMMUNICATIONS ANTENNA 1 3
CHAFF DISPENSER
FUSELAGE FUEL DUMP
RADAR ALTIMETER ANTENNA
BACK UP HYDRAULIC MOTOR PUMP RESERVOIR ASSEMBLY

1 A-6E 158041 THRU 159579 AND A-6E MOD 1 THRU 120

2 A-6E 159895 AND ON AND A-6E MOD 121 AND ON

3 A-6E 158041 THRU 159579 AND A-6E MOD 1 THRU 120 NOT INCORPORATING A.F.C. NO. 300

4 A-6E 158041 THRU 159579 AND A-6E MOD 1 THRU 120 INCORPORATING A.F.C. NO. 161

when the aircraft was. Grumman delivered the TRAM aircraft with a flush plate where the turret was to be located, and for some time A-6E TRAMs were often seen with this plate in place rather than the turret. As the equipment became available, the turrets were added.

The second noticeable change to the TRAM configured Intruders is the rather large air scoop for cooling the aft avionics bay. This scoop is mounted on the top aft fuselage and considerably to the left of centerline. An exhaust port appears on the side of the fuselage below it.

With the TRAM there are also changes made internally that are not visible to the eye. These include a further upgrade to the computer, which is now designated AN/ASQ-155. The AN/ASN-92 Inertial Navigation system replaces the AN/ASN-31, and the AN/APQ-156 radar was installed in place of the AN/APQ-148. The Automatic Carrier Landing System (ACLS), begun with AFC-161 on the A-6E, was standard for all TRAM aircraft. There were other upgrades to the IFF, communications, and navigational equipment, but the table on page 7, referred to earlier, contains a listing of the major changes that were incorpo-

rated. It should also be noted that some equipment, particularly ECM gear, was constantly being upgraded during the A-6 program irrespective of specific model changes.

The same former A-6A airframe, 155673, that had served as the prototype for the A-6E also served as the prototype for the A-6E TRAM. It made its first flight in this configuration on March 22, 1974.

As this is written, another program is underway with the A-6 aircraft, but this program does not involve upgrading the series. Instead, it is more of a life extension program. Because of the increasing number of hours on many A-6 airframes, cracks have developed in the wings. A re-winging program has begun to replace the wings. This effort is underway at present, and will take some time to accomplish. This re-winging is being accomplished by Boeing, and includes a new wing box and spar. Still, new A-6s continue to roll off the assembly line with production now at about six per year. With the A-7F due to start into production in the not-to-distant future, it is a safe bet for Grumman that they will be in the business of producing Intruders well into the 1990s and perhaps beyond.

The more sophisticated A-6E replaced the A-6A as the first line attack version of the Intruder. Some A-6Es were built as such on the production line, and many others were converted from A-6As. This A-6E belongs to Marine squadron VMAT (AW) 202. (Geer)

The A-6E TRAM is an upgraded A-6E. It is recognizable by a small turret under the radome and an extra cooling intake scoop on the aft left fuselage. This aircraft is from VA-85.

A-6E COCKPIT LAYOUT

PILOT'S STATION

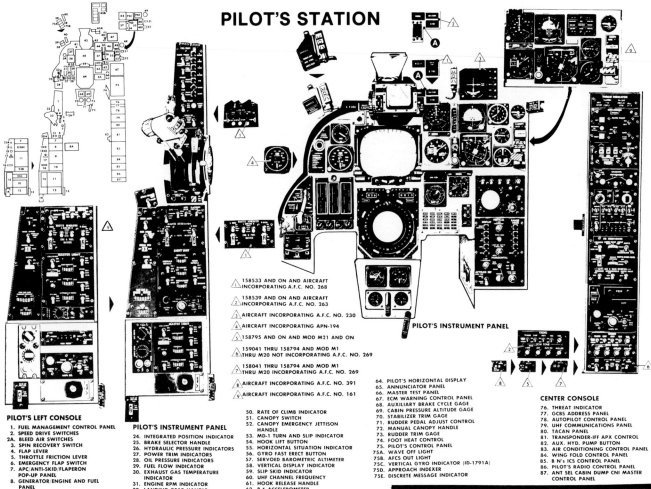

PILOT'S INSTRUMENT PANEL

△ 158533 AND ON AND AIRCRAFT
  INCORPORATING A.F.C. NO. 268

△ 158539 AND ON AND AIRCRAFT
  INCORPORATING A.F.C. NO. 263

△ AIRCRAFT INCORPORATING A.F.C. NO. 230

△ AIRCRAFT INCORPORATING APN-194

△ 158795 AND ON AND MOD M21 AND ON

△ 159041 THRU 158794 AND MOD M1
  THRU M20 NOT INCORPORATING A.F.C. NO. 269

△ 158041 THRU 158794 AND MOD M1
  THRU M20 INCORPORATING A.F.C. NO. 269

△ AIRCRAFT INCORPORATING A.F.C. NO. 391

△ AIRCRAFT INCORPORATING A.F.C. NO. 161

CENTER CONSOLE

PILOT'S LEFT CONSOLE

1. FUEL MANAGEMENT CONTROL PANEL
2. SPEED DRIVE SWITCHES
2A. BLEED AIR SWITCHES
3. SPIN RECOVERY SWITCH
4. FLAP LEVER
5. THROTTLE FRICTION LEVER
6. EMERGENCY FLAP SWITCH
7. APC ANTI-SKID/FLAPERON POP-UP PANEL
8. GENERATOR/ENGINE AND FUEL PANEL
8A. GENERATOR/SPEED DRIVE/ENGINE AND FUEL PANEL
9. SIGHT UNIT CONTROL PANEL
10. PILOT'S ICS PANEL
11. MASTER LIGHT CONTROL PANEL
12. G-VALVE TEST BUTTON
13. RAM AIR TURBINE HANDLE
14. BACK-UP HYDRAULIC SYSTEM TEST SWITCH
15. AUXILIARY UHF RECEIVER PANEL
16. VENT SUIT-SEAT CUSHION CONTROL
17. OXYGEN SWITCH
18. RUDDER TRIM SWITCH
19. ARRESTING HOOK POSITION WARNING BY-PASS SWITCH
20. SPEED BRAKE TEST SWITCH
21. CRANK SWITCHES
22. THROTTLES
23. CATAPULT GRIP
23A. VGI DIS SWITCH
23B. ARA-63 CONTROL PANEL
23C. ASW-25 CONTROL PANEL

PILOT'S INSTRUMENT PANEL

24. INTEGRATED POSITION INDICATOR
25. BRAKE SELECTOR HANDLE
26. HYDRAULIC PRESSURE INDICATORS
27. POWER TRIM INDICATORS
28. OIL PRESSURE INDICATORS
29. FUEL FLOW INDICATOR
30. EXHAUST GAS TEMPERATURE INDICATOR
31. ENGINE RPM INDICATOR
32. LANDING GEAR INDICATOR
33. LANDING GEAR OVERRIDE HANDLE
34. EMERGENCY STORES JETTISON BUTTON
35. LOW ALTITUDE WARNING LAMB
36. RADAR ALTIMETER
37. ANGLE OF ATTACK INDICATOR
38. APCS STANDBY LIGHT
39. WHEELS WARNING LIGHT
40. APPROACH INDEXER
41. MASTER CAUTION RESET BUTTON
42. OPTICAL SIGHT
43. DECM CONTROL PANEL
43A. NWW TEMP LIGHT
43B. WARNING LIGHT PANEL/THREAT STATUS
44. MACH/AIR SPEED INDICATOR
45. 'G' METER
46. VERTICAL GYRO INDICATOR
47. ACLS INDICATOR
48. CLOCK
49. OXYGEN QUANTITY GAGE

50. RATE OF CLIMB INDICATOR
51. CANOPY SWITCH
52. CANOPY EMERGENCY JETTISON HANDLE
53. MD-1 TURN AND SLIP INDICATOR
54. HOOK LIFT BUTTON
55. HORIZONTAL SITUATION INDICATOR
56. GYRO FAST ERECT BUTTON
57. SERVOED BAROMETRIC ALTIMETER
58. VERTICAL DISPLAY INDICATOR
59. SLIP SKID INDICATOR
60. UHF CHANNEL FREQUENCY
61. HOOK RELEASE HANDLE
62. B-6 ACCELEROMETER
63. FUEL QUANTITY GAGE

64. PILOT'S HORIZONTAL DISPLAY
65. ANNUNCIATOR PANEL
66. MASTER TEST PANEL
67. ECM WARNING CONTROL PANEL
68. AUXILIARY BRAKE CYCLE GAGE
69. CABIN PRESSURE ALTITUDE GAGE
70. STABILIZER TRIM GAGE
71. RUDDER PEDAL ADJUST CONTROL
72. MANUAL CANOPY HANDLE
73. RUDDER TRIM GAGE
74. FOOT HEAT CONTROL
75. PILOT'S CONTROL PANEL
75A. WAVE OFF LIGHT
75B. AFCS OUT LIGHT
75C. VERTICAL GYRO INDICATOR (ID-1791A)
75D. APPROACH INDEXER
75E. DISCRETE MESSAGE INDICATOR

CENTER CONSOLE

76. THREAT INDICATOR
77. GCBS ADDRESS PANEL
78. AUTOPILOT CONTROL PANEL
79. UHF COMMUNICATIONS PANEL
80. TACAN PANEL
81. TRANSPONDER-IFF APX CONTROL
82. AUX. HYD. PUMP BUTTON
83. AIR CONDITIONING CONTROL PANEL
84. WING FOLD CONTROL PANEL
85. B N's ICS CONTROL PANEL
86. PILOT'S RADIO CONTROL PANEL
87. ANT SEL CABIN DUMP CNI MASTER CONTROL PANEL

BOMBARDIER'S STATION

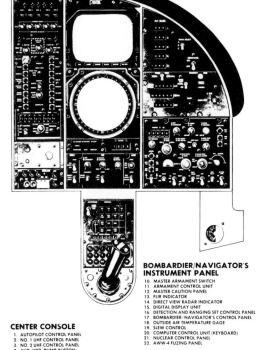

BOMBARDIER/NAVIGATOR'S INSTRUMENT PANEL

10. MASTER ARMAMENT SWITCH
11. ARMAMENT CONTROL UNIT
12. MASTER CAUTION PANEL
13. FLIR INDICATOR
14. DIRECT VIEW RADAR INDICATOR
15. DIGITAL DISPLAY UNIT
16. DETECTION AND RANGING SET CONTROL PANEL
17. BOMBARDIER/NAVIGATOR'S CONTROL PANEL
18. OUTSIDE AIR TEMPERATURE GAGE
19. SLEW CONTROL
20. COMPUTER CONTROL UNIT (KEYBOARD)
21. NUCLEAR CONTROL PANEL
22. AWW-4 FUZING PANEL

CENTER CONSOLE

1. AUTOPILOT CONTROL PANEL
2. NO. 1 UHF CONTROL PANEL
3. NO. 2 UHF CONTROL PANEL
4. AUX. HYD. PUMP BUTTON
5. TACAN CONTROL PANEL
6. IFF/SIF TRANSPONDER CONTROL
7. WING FOLD PANEL
8. AIR CONDITIONING CONTROL PANEL
9. CABIN DUMP/MA-1/ADC PANEL

BOMBARDIER/NAVIGATOR'S RIGHT CONSOLE

23. RADAR/DRS TEST PANEL
24. CONDOR CONTROL PANEL
25. ECM PANEL
26. VIDEO TAPE RECORDER
27. DOPPLER CONTROL PANEL
28. NAVIGATION CONTROL PANEL
29. RADIO/ICS CONTROL PANEL
30. CHAFF DISPENSER CONTROL PANEL
31. OXYGEN LEVER
32. MASTER TEST BUTTON
33. INTERIOR LIGHTING CONTROL PANEL
34. VENT SUIT-SEAT CUSHION CONTROL
35. G-VALVE TEST BUTTON
36. CLOCK

AFT BULKHEAD CONSOLE

37. RADAR BEACON CONTROL PANEL
38. KY-28 CONTROL PANEL
39. MA-1 COMPASS CONTROL PANEL

A-6E TRAM COCKPIT LAYOUT

PILOT'S STATION

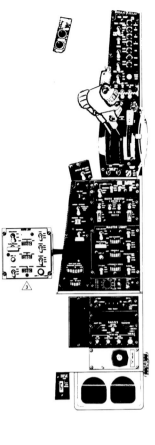

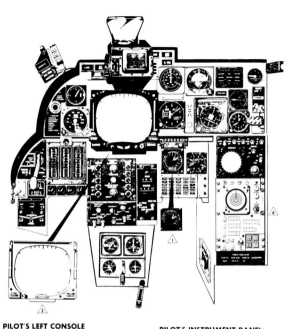

PILOT'S LEFT CONSOLE

1. FUEL MANAGEMENT CONTROL PANEL
2. BLEED AIR SWITCHES
3. SPIN RECOVERY SWITCH
4. FLAP LEVER
5. THROTTLE FRICTION LEVER
6. EMERGENCY FLAP SWITCH
7. APC/ANTI SKID/FLAPERON POP UP PANEL
8. GENERATOR/SPEED DRIVE/ENGINE AND FUEL PANEL
9. MASTER LIGHT PANEL
10. ILS RECEIVER CONTROL PANEL
11. ACLS CONTROL PANEL
12. RADIO/ICS CONTROL PANEL
13. G VALVE TEST BUTTON
14. RAM AIR TURBINE HANDLE
15. BACK-UP HYDRAULIC SYSTEM TEST SWITCH
16. VENT SUIT/SEAT CUSHION CONTROL
17. OXYGEN SWITCH
18. RUDDER TRIM SWITCH
19. ARRESTING HOOK POSITION WARNING BY PASS SWITCH
20. SPEED BRAKE TEST SWITCH
21. CRANK SWITCHES
22. THROTTLES
23. CATAPULT GRIP
24. CANOPY BOW PANEL

PILOT'S INSTRUMENT PANEL

25. INTEGRATED POSITION INDICATOR
26. BRAKE SELECTOR HANDLE
27. HYDRAULIC PRESSURE INDICATORS
28. POWER TRIM INDICATORS
29. OIL PRESSURE INDICATORS
30. FUEL FLOW INDICATOR
31. EXHAUST GAS TEMPERATURE INDICATOR
32. ENGINE RPM INDICATOR
33. LANDING GEAR HANDLE
34. LANDING GEAR OVERRIDE HANDLE
35. EMERGENCY STORES JETTISON BUTTON
36. LOW ALTITUDE WARNING LIGHT
37. RADAR ALTIMETER (AN/APN 143 OR AN/APN 194)
38. ANGLE OF ATTACK INDICATOR
39. AFCS OUT INDICATOR LIGHT
40. APC STBY INDICATOR LIGHT
41. WAVE OFF INDICATOR LIGHT
42. WHEELS WARNING LIGHT
43. APPROACH INDEXER
44. LEFT FIRE WARNING LIGHT
45. AFT TEMP WARNING LIGHT
46. MASTER CAUTION LIGHT
47. OPTICAL SIGHT

CENTER CONSOLE

81. AUTOPILOT CONTROL PANEL
82. NO. 1 UHF CONTROL PANEL
83. NO. 2 UHF CONTROL PANEL
84. AUX. HYD. PUMP BUTTON
85. TACAN CONTROL PANEL
86. IFF/SIF TRANSPONDER CONTROL
87. WING FOLD PANEL
88. AIR CONDITIONING CONTROL PANEL
89. CABIN DUMP/MA.1/ADC PANEL

⚠ 1 AIRCRAFT WITH AVC 1870

⚠ 2 A-6E TRAM 160955 AND ON, M215 AND ON

⚠ 3 A-6E TRAM 161092 AND ON

⚠ 4 A-6E TRAM 152645 (TR 17), 155604 (TR 20), 158529 (TR 15), 158746 (TR 16), 158797 (TR 18), 159311 (TR 23), 159314 (TR 22) AND 159574 (TR 25) ONLY

BOMBARDIER'S STATION

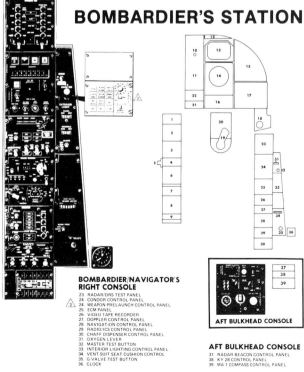

CENTER CONSOLE

1. AUTOPILOT CONTROL PANEL
2. NO. 1 UHF CONTROL PANEL
3. NO. 2 UHF CONTROL PANEL
4. AUX. HYD. PUMP BUTTON
5. TACAN CONTROL PANEL
6. IFF/SIF TRANSPONDER CONTROL
7. WING FOLD PANEL
8. AIR CONDITIONING CONTROL PANEL
9. CABIN DUMP/MA.1/ADC PANEL

⚠ 1 A-6E TRAM 159895 THRU 159906 AND M121 THRU M161

⚠ 2 A-6E TRAM 160421 AND ON, AND M162 AND ON

⚠ 3 A-6E TRAM 152645 (TR 17), 155604 (TR 20), 158529 (TR 15), 158796 (TR 16), 158797 (TR 18), 159311 (TR 23), 159314 (TR 22) AND 159574 (TR 25)

BOMBARDIER/NAVIGATOR'S INSTRUMENT PANEL

10. MASTER ARMAMENT SWITCH
11. ARMAMENT CONTROL UNIT
12. MASTER CAUTION PANEL
13. FLIR INDICATOR
14. DIRECT VIEW RADAR INDICATOR
15. DIGITAL DISPLAY UNIT
16. DETECTION AND RANGING SET CONTROL PANEL
17. BOMBARDIER/NAVIGATOR'S CONTROL PANEL
18. OUTSIDE AIR TEMPERATURE GAGE
19. SLEW CONTROL
20. COMPUTER CONTROL UNIT (KEYBOARD)
21. NUCLEAR CONTROL PANEL
22. AWW-4 FUZING PANEL

BOMBARDIER/NAVIGATOR'S RIGHT CONSOLE

23. RADAR/DRS TEST PANEL
24. CONDOR CONTROL UNIT
24. WEAPON PRELAUNCH CONTROL PANEL
25. ECM PANEL
26. VIDEO TAPE RECORDER
27. DOPPLER CONTROL PANEL
28. NAVIGATION CONTROL PANEL
29. RADIO/ICS CONTROL PANEL
30. CHAFF DISPENSER CONTROL PANEL
31. OXYGEN LEVER
32. MASTER TEST BUTTON
33. INTERIOR LIGHTING CONTROL PANEL
34. VENT SUIT SEAT CUSHION CONTROL
35. G VALVE TEST BUTTON
36. CLOCK

AFT BULKHEAD CONSOLE

37. RADAR BEACON CONTROL PANEL
38. KY 28
39. MA 1 COMPASS CONTROL PANEL

EQUIPMENT CAGE

An extendable equipment cage is standard on attack versions of the A-6. It is located under the fuselage just forward of the tail hook. These four photographs show details of the cage on an A-6E TRAM.

TRAM MODIFICATIONS

The most noticeable feature about the TRAM modification is the turret added below the radome. TRAM aircraft are delivered from Grumman with a flush plate where the turret is to go, and the turret is added when the equipment is available. A-6E TRAMs are often seen with the plate, but not the turret, in place. These three views show details of the turret.

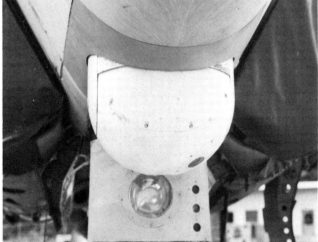

A new scoop was added to the top aft fuselage on the left side. This provided air-conditioning for new equipment located in this part of the aircraft. The exhaust port for the system is visible under the national insignia in the photo at right.

KA-6D TANKER

The KA-6D is the dedicated tanker version of the Intruder design. This excellent taxi shot shows the slats, flaps, and spoilers on the wings to good effect.

(Cockle)

Obtaining a suitable carrier-borne aerial tanker has always been a problem for the Navy, and it has always been solved to a greater or lesser degree by modifying aircraft originally intended for other missions. It would be nice to have a big tanker with KC-135 capabilities that could orbit and refuel numerous aircraft for long periods of time. But such an aircraft simply would not fit on even the largest of carriers.

In April 1966, Grumman demonstrated the tanker capability of the A-6 by using a modified A-6A, 149937, to in-flight refuel an F-4 Phantom. But the Navy was less than enthusiastic at the time. However, by 1969, the Navy had changed its mind, and it placed an order for KA-6D tanker versions. These aircraft were all former A-6As which had their aft equipment cages removed and replaced with a hose and reel refueling system. The all-weather avionics equipment was deleted, leaving the right side of the cockpit rather bare with the removal of the associated displays and controls. Although the KA-6D was to retain a clear weather bombing capability, LT Goodman, when questioned about this, stated that the panels were there, but he had never seen any that worked. He stated that practice bombing was not done in KA-6Ds. However, the five external fuel tanks could be dropped if necessary.

The refueling system can transfer fuel at a rate up to 350 gallons per minute, and a maximum of about 3000 gallons are transferable. This includes fuel in the internal tanks and five external 300-gallon tanks which are almost always seen on a KA-6D. The first KA-6D, other than the original demonstration aircraft, was BuNo. 151582, which made its first flight on April 16, 1970.

The KA-6D initially deployed with VA-176 in 1971, as that unit took the tanker to Vietnam with its A-6As. Normally, four or five tankers are mixed with eight or nine attack versions, but the numbers do vary, and when two A-6 squadrons deploy aboard a carrier in a dual A-6 wing, only one squadron has tankers, and the other has only bombers. When VA-85 deployed in the dual A-6 air wing for the cruise during which LT Goodman was shot down, they had thirteen aircraft, all of which were A-6E TRAMs. VA-75 had the bomber/tanker mix on that cruise.

Actually any attack version of the A-6 can operate as a tanker through the use of a "buddy" refueling store carried on the centerline station. With this capability, why was a dedicated tanker version needed? Why not have squadrons equipped entirely with aircraft with full attack capability, and use them as needed for tankers? These questions were posed to LT Goodman, and he explained that at the time the KA-6D was ordered, the "buddy" system was not as reliable as it should be. The system on the KA-6D worked exceptionally well, and when an aircraft needed gas was no time to have problems with the refueling system. It should also be noted that the "buddy" store occupied the centerline station which otherwise could be used to carry a full three-hundred gallon tank.

About the only noticeable difference in the physical appearance of a KA-6D, as opposed to an attack version, is the fairing under the aft fuselage for the refueling drogue and hose. To help pilots pick out a tanker in flight, KA-6Ds often had a fuselage band painted in the squadron color, and was located just forward of the horizontal tail. This was a standard practice in the gray-over-white paint scheme (a scheme generally worn for a much longer period of time by the tankers than the attack versions), but with the newer subdued tactical schemes, this band is often deleted. When carried, it is usually painted in some low visibility gray color. At night, a tanker can be distinguished by the green light at the leading edge of the vertical tail. The light is red on attack versions. As photographs were being taken for this publication, it was noticed that an Omega blade antenna had been recently added to KA-6Ds just behind the canopy. This antenna did not appear on A-6E TRAMs.

KA-6D GENERAL ARRANGEMENT

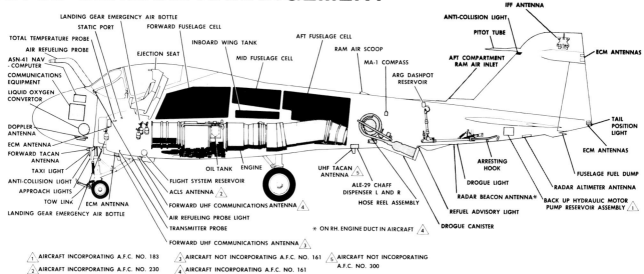

IFF ANTENNA
ANTI-COLLISION LIGHT
PITOT TUBE
LANDING GEAR EMERGENCY AIR BOTTLE
STATIC PORT
FORWARD FUSELAGE CELL
TOTAL TEMPERATURE PROBE
AIR REFUELING PROBE
INBOARD WING TANK
AFT FUSELAGE CELL
ECM ANTENNAS
ASN-41 NAV - COMPUTER
EJECTION SEAT
MID FUSELAGE CELL
RAM AIR SCOOP
COMMUNICATIONS EQUIPMENT
MA-1 COMPASS
AFT COMPARTMENT RAM AIR INLET
LIQUID OXYGEN CONVERTOR
ARG DASHPOT RESERVOIR
TAIL POSITION LIGHT
DOPPLER ANTENNA
ECM ANTENNA
ECM ANTENNAS
FORWARD TACAN ANTENNA
ARRESTING HOOK
FUSELAGE FUEL DUMP
TAXI LIGHT
OIL TANK
ENGINE
UHF TACAN ANTENNA 5
DROGUE LIGHT
RADAR ALTIMETER ANTENNA
ANTI-COLLISION LIGHT
FLIGHT SYSTEM RESERVOIR
APPROACH LIGHTS
ACLS ANTENNA 2
ALE-29 CHAFF DISPENSER L AND R
RADAR BEACON ANTENNA *
BACK UP HYDRAULIC MOTOR PUMP RESERVOIR ASSEMBLY 1
TOW LINK
ECM ANTENNA
FORWARD UHF COMMUNICATIONS ANTENNA 4
HOSE REEL ASSEMBLY
REFUEL ADVISORY LIGHT
LANDING GEAR EMERGENCY AIR BOTTLE
AIR REFUELING PROBE LIGHT
DROGUE CANISTER
TRANSMITTER PROBE
* ON RH. ENGINE DUCT IN AIRCRAFT 4
FORWARD UHF COMMUNICATIONS ANTENNA 3

1 AIRCRAFT INCORPORATING A.F.C. NO. 183
3 AIRCRAFT NOT INCORPORATING A.F.C. NO. 161
5 AIRCRAFT NOT INCORPORATING A.F.C. NO. 300
2 AIRCRAFT INCORPORATING A.F.C. NO. 230
4 AIRCRAFT INCORPORATING A.F.C. NO. 161

KA-6Ds now have an omega antenna added to the spine just behind the cockpit. It is used for navigation. It was not originally seen here on tanker versions, and is not on the attack versions.

Left: Tankers are usually seen with external fuel tanks on all pylons. But as seen in the photo at the top of the previous page, a buddy refueling store is sometimes carried on the centerline station. The buddy store provides the capability for any A-6 to act as a tanker. (Cockle)

A small air scoop is seen on the spine of the KA-6D, as is a small black box. The lights on the vertical tail are green on tankers and red on attack versions.

KA-6D COCKPIT LAYOUT

PILOT'S STATION

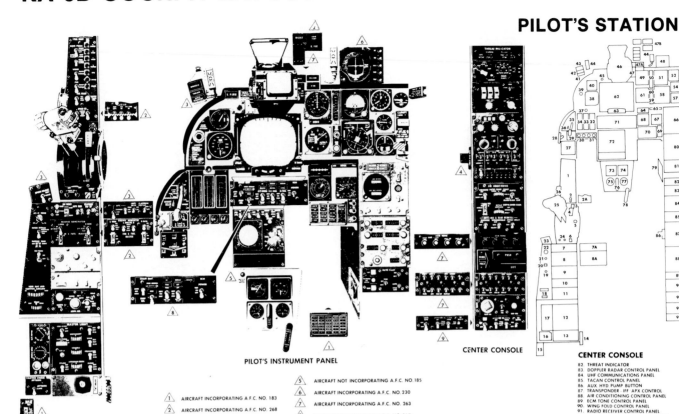

PILOT'S INSTRUMENT PANEL

CENTER CONSOLE

PILOT'S LEFT CONSOLE

CENTER CONSOLE

△1 AIRCRAFT INCORPORATING A.F.C. NO. 183
△2 AIRCRAFT INCORPORATING A.F.C. NO. 268
△3 AIRCRAFT INCORPORATING A.F.C. NO. 199
△4 INCORPORATING A.F.C. NO. 185

△5 AIRCRAFT NOT INCORPORATING A.F.C. NO. 185
△6 AIRCRAFT INCORPORATING A.F.C. NO. 230
△7 AIRCRAFT INCORPORATING A.F.C. NO. 263
△8 AIRCRAFT INCORPORATING A.F.C. NO. 287
△9 INCORPORATING A.F.C. NO. 269

PILOT'S LEFT CONSOLE
1. FUEL MANAGEMENT CONTROL PANEL
2. SPEED DRIVE SWITCHES
2A BLEED AIR SWITCHES
3. SPIN RECOVERY SWITCH
4. FLAP LEVER
5. THROTTLE FRICTION LEVER
6. EMERGENCY FLAP SWITCH
7. SPEED BRAKE/UHF PRESET/ANTI-SKID
   FLAPERON POP-UP PANEL
7A APC/ANTI-SKID/FLAPERON POP-UP PANEL
8. MASTER GENERATOR/ENGINE AND FUEL
   MASTER CONTROL PANEL
8A MASTER GENERATOR/SPEED DRIVE/ENGINE
   AND FUEL MASTER CONTROL

11. ICS CONTROL PANEL
12. MASTER LIGHT CONTROL PANEL
13. G VALVE TEST BUTTON
14. RAM AIR TURBINE HANDLE
15. BACK-UP HYDRAULIC SYSTEM TEST SWITCH
16. SELECTIVE STORES JETTISON SWITCH
17. AUXILIARY UHF RECEIVER PANEL
18. VENT SUIT SEAT CUSHION CONTROL PANEL
19. OXYGEN SWITCH
20. RUDDER TRIM SWITCH
21. HOOK BYPASS SWITCH
22. ICI - R TONE CONTROL
23. SPEED BRAKE TEST SWITCH
24. CRANK SWITCHES
25. THROTTLES
26. CATAPULT GRIP

PILOT'S INSTRUMENT PANEL
27. INTEGRATED POSITION INDICATOR
28. BRAKE SELECTOR HANDLE
29. HYDRAULIC PRESSURE INDICATORS
30. POWER TRIM INDICATORS
31. OIL PRESSURE INDICATORS
32. FUEL FLOW INDICATOR
33. EXHAUST GAS TEMPERATURE INDICATOR
34. ENGINE RPM INDICATOR
35. LANDING GEAR HANDLE
36. LANDING GEAR OVERRIDE LEVER
37. LOW ALTITUDE WARNING LIGHT
38. RADAR ALTIMETER
39. EMERGENCY STORES JETTISON BUTTON
40. ANGLE-OF-ATTACK INDICATOR
41. APCS STANDBY LIGHT
42. TACAN LIGHT
43. WHEELS WARNING LIGHT
44. APPROACH INDEXER
45. MASTER CAUTION RESET BUTTON

46. OPTICAL SIGHT
47. DECM CONTROL PANEL
47A COLLISION LIGHT
47B WARNING LIGHT PANEL
48. ACLS INDICATOR
49. MACH/AIR SPEED INDICATOR
50. G METER
51. VERTICAL GYRO INDICATOR
52. CLOCK
53. OXYGEN QUANTITY GAGE
54. RATE OF CLIMB INDICATOR
55. CANOPY SWITCH
56. CANOPY EMERGENCY JETTISON HANDLE
57. TURN AND SLIP INDICATOR
58. HORIZONTAL SITUATION INDICATOR
59. GYRO FAST ERECT BUTTON
60. HOOK LIFT BUTTON
61. COUNTER/POINTER ALTIMETER
62. VERTICAL DISPLAY INDICATOR
63. SLIP/SKID INDICATOR
64. UHF CHANNEL/FREQUENCY

65. HOOK RELEASE HANDLE
66. REFUEL CONTROL PANEL
67. ACCELEROMETER
68. FUEL QUANTITY GAGE
69. MASTER TEST PANEL
70. ANNUNCIATOR PANEL
71. ECM CONTROL PANEL
72. APR 25 CONTROL PANEL
73. AUXILIARY BRAKE CYCLE GAGE
74. CABIN PRESSURE ALTITUDE GAGE
75. STABILIZER TRIM GAGE
76. RUDDER PEDAL ADJUST CONTROL
77. RUDDER TRIM GAGE
78. MANUAL CANOPY HANDLE
79. FOOT HEAT CONTROL
80. NAVIGATION CONTROL PANEL
81. AUTOPILOT CONTROL PANEL

CENTER CONSOLE
82. THREAT INDICATOR
83. DOPPLER RADAR CONTROL PANEL
84. UHF COMMUNICATIONS PANEL
85. TACAN CONTROL PANEL
86. AUX. HYD. PUMP BUTTON
87. TRANSPONDER · IFF · APX CONTROL
88. AIR CONDITIONING CONTROL PANEL
89. ECM TONE CONTROL PANEL
90. WING FOLD CONTROL PANEL
91. RADIO RECEIVER CONTROL PANEL
92. RADIO TRANSMITTER CONTROL PANEL
93. CABIN DUMP · ANT SEL · CNI MASTER
    CONTROL PANEL

BOMBARDIER'S STATION

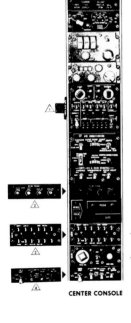
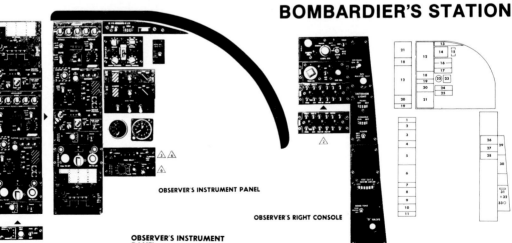
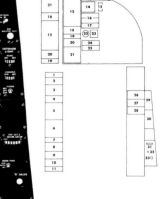

OBSERVER'S INSTRUMENT PANEL

OBSERVER'S RIGHT CONSOLE

CENTER CONSOLE

CENTER CONSOLE
1. THREAT INDICATOR
2. DOPPLER RADAR CONTROL PANEL
3. UHF COMMUNICATIONS PANEL
4. TRANSPONDER - IFF / APX CONTROL
5. AIR CONDITIONING CONTROL PANEL
6. ECM TONE CONTROL PANEL
7. WING FOLD CONTROL PANEL
8. RADIO RECEIVER CONTROL PANEL
9. RADIO TRANSMITTER CONTROL PANEL
10. RADIO TRANSMITTER CONTROL PANEL
11. CABIN DUMP/ANT SEL/CNI MASTER CONTROL
    PANEL

OBSERVER'S INSTRUMENT PANEL
12. ARMAMENT CONTROL PANEL
13. ICI-R COOLING CONTROL PANEL
14. CHAFF DISPENSER CONTROL PANEL
15. HOSE REEL GROUND TEST PANEL
16. KY-28 CONTROL PANELS (2)
17. MISCELLANEOUS TONE CONTROL PANEL
18. CENTER LINE STORE CONTROL PANEL
19. RADAR BEACON CONTROL PANEL
20. MA-1 COMPASS CONTROL PANEL
21. UHF NO. 2 COMMUNICATIONS CONTROL PANEL
22. OUTSIDE AIR TEMPERATURE GAGE
23. CLOCK
24. ACLS CONTROL PANEL
25. ILS CONTROL PANEL

OBSERVER'S RIGHT CONSOLE
26. ICS CONTROL PANEL
27. RADIO TRANSMITTER SELECTOR PANEL
28. RADIO RECEIVER SELECTOR PANEL
29. OXYGEN SWITCH
30. INTERIOR LIGHTING CONTROL PANEL
31. VENT SUIT/SEAT CUSHION CONTROL
32. BOMB TONE SWITCH
33. G-VALVE TEST BUTTON

△1 AIRCRAFT INCORPORATING AFC NO. 185
△2 AIRCRAFT INCORPORATING AFC NO. 263
△3 AIRCRAFT INCORPORATING AFC NO. 230
△4 AIRCRAFT INCORPORATING AFC NO. 269
△5 AIRCRAFT INCORPORATING AFC NO. 299
△6 AIRCRAFT INCORPORATING AFC NO. 161

These four photos show the drogue refueling system on a KA-6D. It is located in the same place as the equipment cage on an attack version, but is hinged at the front rather than the rear.

LT GOODMAN'S STORY

VA-85 personnel pose with one of their aircraft on the cruise in which the action over Lebanon took place. LT Goodman is third from the left in the front row. LT Mark Lange is seventh from the left in the standing row. LT Lange was the pilot paired with LT Goodman, and he lost his life on the mission when their aircraft was shot down.   (VA-85)

LT Robert Goodman, USN.   (Goodman)

Note: LT Robert Goodman made headlines when his A-6E TRAM was shot down over Lebanon on December 4, 1983. He was held captive by the Syrians until being released, after which he returned home on January 4, 1984. His pilot, LT Mark Lange was killed when the aircraft was shot down.

LT Goodman was born in San Juan, Puerto Rico, in 1956, and is a 1978 graduate of the U.S. Naval Academy. Here, for the first time publicly, LT Goodman takes a look back at the mission and his captivity. His narrative is interesting, exciting, and informative, allowing the reader to get inside the thoughts of a naval aviator during his training, his first combat, and his captivity.

The author spent two days with LT Goodman in May 1984. While most of the military people I have worked with gathering information for my aviation writing have been very friendly and helpful, LT Goodman was the most personable I have known. He did not simply work with me as though it was part of his job to do so, but instead he treated me as a friend that he could not do enough for. Considering that LT Goodman had just received so much press coverage, and had to accommodate many people from the various forms of media, it was remarkable that he was so willing to patiently spend so much time (much of it his own) with yet another person that wanted to learn more about an experience he would probably just as soon forget. But instead, he acted as if he had known me all of his life. Not only did he make every attempt to get all of the information on the A-6 that I wanted, he also displayed a genuine friendliness. Other reports have credited him with intelligence, optimism, sense of humor, and a level head. Those reports are not exaggerated. LT Goodman impressed me, as he would anyone, as being a truly fine human being. This personal note here is only to relate the impression that such a fine person can make. Once having spent some time with LT Goodman, anyone would understand why he represented himself and his country with dignity and honor during the most trying of circumstances. Here then in his own words is his story -- how he felt about "The Real Thing."

Two VA-85 aircraft are seen on a training mission prior to the cruise where the unit saw action over Lebanon. (VA-85)

THE REAL THING

During my relatively short naval aviation career, spanning approximately six years from Naval Aviation Schools Command through my first squadron tour, the emphasis had always been directed toward the eventuality of combat -- The Real Thing. This emphasis took the form of practicing, exercising, studying, simulating, training, maintaining, and operating -- all in preparation for The Real Thing.

My experience level in Attack Squadron Eight Five was somewhat median as far as seniority and experience were concerned. I had over 750 hours in the A-6, over 1100 hours of total flight time, and 276 arrested carrier landings (of which 112 were at night) aboard the USS JOHN F. KENNEDY and the USS FORRESTAL. This would have been my second extended cruise. My jobs in VA-85 have included Educational Services Officer, Line Division Officer, and B/N Natops Officer.

This particular cruise had already been somewhat unique from our squadron's standpoint. A typical A-6 squadron will deploy with a mix of A-6E bombers, and KA-6D tankers. When VA-85 was assigned to the dual A-6 air wing aboard the USS KENNEDY (as opposed to the standard mix of one A-6 and two A-7 squadrons) we deployed with thirteen A-6Es and no tankers. The other A-6 squadron provided the tankers for the air wing. This meant that on every flight a bombardier/navigator (B/N) would get valuable system time, building confidence and proficiency versus the usual 40/60 split of that valuable time, spending the sixty percent in the systemless KA-6D version.

This particular mission was a retaliation against Syrian anti-aircraft positions which had fired on F-14 reconnaissance flights from Carrier Air Wings Three and Six. It was not the first time these flights had been fired upon. However, after the incident on December 3, it was decided to respond with an airstrike. Although much has been made of the short time frame in which events proceeded on this strike, an atmosphere developed in the weeks prior to it in which every flightcrew member was aware of the possibility

of going over the beach. I personally felt very comfortable with that possibility from the exercise standpoint. An atmosphere develops during these situations that is somewhat hard to explain to the uninitiated general public. Naval aviators as a group are not by nature warmongers, although they may try to give that impression in an O'club. If you have listened to the sea stories of the Vietnam veterans who are still in our active ranks at the squadron level, they alone have the most accurate picture of war. While the reality of war is foremost in any naval aviator's mind, they, as a group, will not hesitate to test their mettle in any combat situation. Thus, when the possibility of an airstrike presented itself, everyone, including myself, was anxious to be involved in some capacity.

I was awakened by a roommate at 0430 on December 4, and told to go to the planning room to make preparations for the strike. When I arrived, I was given the details of my target, ordnance load, formation, place in the flight, route of flight, and other essentials. I was told that I would be crewed with Mark (LT Lange). Mark and I were not currently crewed together, but had been in the past. He was a good pilot who held a reputation for being an excellent manual dive bomber pilot. My reactions to the circumstances were as if it was another contingency planning exercise -- planning and preparing in earnest, but feeling deep down that this was another "planex." Very soon it was evident that something more was at stake than just missing breakfast. At approximately 0600, the word was passed that the strike would launch at 0730. Even at that time I was unsure whether I would go because of the aircraft assignments. I was slated for aircraft 556 which had no ordnance loaded. Because of the short time frame, there was a question as to whether the aircraft would be armed in time. At my point of involvement, I was interested only in spending the short time remaining trying to ensure that I could do the best job I could, and to prepare myself for any eventualities that might arise.

The Air Wing Commander, who was flying in one of our aircraft, conducted a formal briefing of the finalized plan.

This is A-6E TRAM, 152915, which was the Intruder crewed by LT Mark Lange and LT Bob Goodman when it was lost on December 4, 1983. Although taken at some distance, and not being of the highest quality, it is the only photograph that we have found of the aircraft that shows the markings it carried at the time it was shot down. It is in the overall tactical blue-gray (FS 36320) scheme, with light gray (approximately FS 36375) markings. The 556 nose number is flat black. Detail & Scale was able to research these markings using the log book for the actual aircraft, and we found that VA-85's A-6s were not painted in the two-tone tactical scheme used on many Intruders. This aircraft was originally built as an A-6A, then converted to A-6E and later A-6E TRAM configurations.

(U.S. Navy via Campbell)

Afterwards, I dressed in all of my flight gear and returned to the ready room to draw a pistol and ten rounds of ammunition. It was more for moral support than for real protection. The big joke going around the squadron was that the pistol wasn't really worth much if you had to hit a target, but it could always be used to shoot yourself before they did. Pistols are not normally stored in the ready room. When they were brought from the armory to the ready room during the week prior, and carried on some previous flights that neared the beach, I knew the situation had progressed past the exercise stage.

Most of the crews then proceeded directly to the flight deck to man their aircraft. I stayed in the ready room waiting for the word that 556 was completely loaded and would be able to make the launch. At approximately 0710, I was told to go man 556 as a go aircraft. I grabbed my gear as well as Mark's, and hustled to the flight deck. Mark was already on the flight deck helping preflight other aircraft. We preflighted ours, and manned up. Ordnance men were just finishing the loading and fusing of our ordnance which consisted of six Mk-83 2000 pound bombs. A weapons system trouble shooter had the system going and ready. By now the flight deck was uncommonly clear of aircraft, most of which were already in the air. We were the last aircraft that needed to be launched.

My mind was racing, trying to think of all of the things that had to be covered, and the items that I had forgotten. When we taxied out of spot I remember looking down on several people standing around the aircraft and showing them a thumbs up and a crossed fingers good luck sign. We taxied to cat 2 and were launched in time to rendevous with our element in the last turn prior to heading outbound.

After we had joined with our flight, I had my first opportunity to take a deep breath and try to calm the rush of adrenalin in an attempt to comprehend that this was The Real Thing! -- the climax of everything that I had been taught from my very first day at the academy.

As we approached our coast in point, I could hear Captain Andrews broadcasting on the strike frequency. "I've been hit, I'm getting out." (Captain Andrews was shot down while flying an A-7 on the mission.) I never saw his aircraft since it was behind us going outbound as we were going in. As number three in the flight, my main concern was not navigation, but being a lookout. In trying to cover my area of responsibility, I could not help being temporarily paralyzed at seeing the popcorn AAA and a missile trail far aft that extended higher than our aircraft. Shortly afterwards we were hit by another missile that I did not see. I remember the aircraft violently jolting forward and nose down. My eyes immediately went forward to see only ground. My only and last thought was that I've been hit and I should eject. I'm not sure even now if I blacked out and somehow accidently pulled the handle, or if I was alert, but my subconscious mind prevents me from recalling what happened next. I do know that I do not remember pulling the handle to eject. There is a lapse in my memory which resumes with me lying on the ground, my hands being tied, my eyes covered, my watch and wedding ring taken, and my flight gear being taken off my body. I was then placed in a jeep and transported. During this ride I was paraded or shown off at several points along the journey. I was not aware of my various injuries which included broken ribs, a separated shoulder, and a badly bruised left knee. These were all relatively minor considering aircraft speed and probable nose down attitude at the time of ejection. At this point my only concern was my fingers. My hands were tied so tightly that I could feel my fingers and thumbs going numb. These events happened so quickly, and in my semi-conscious state I thought for sure that I was dreaming.

When the truck arrived at its final destination, I was placed in a cell constructed of cement with one small window in the door and a small light bulb on the wall. The cell was approximately five feet square with a ceiling six feet high. The floor was covered with three very heavy blankets that were almost the weight of rugs. My captors had taken all of my clothing and equipment except my underwear and my squadron teeshirt. At this point I started to realize that I had some injuries. My hands had been untied so that I was no longer concerned for my fingers. I did have a great difficulty breathing caused by the broken ribs, and standing or walking because of the bruised knee. As the pain set in I emerged from a sort of fog or shock and realized that I was not dreaming. As this happened, a sense of extreme bitterness hit me. How could the Navy (leadership that I trusted) place me in this situation of trying to solve problems thousands of miles from my home, intruding on people who may not want our help, with problems that have been brewing for years, and trying to solve those problems with ordnance? Now here I am for I don't know how long, and they can do whatever they want with me. I had not assigned in my own mind a nationality to my TGT -- it was merely a TGT to destroy and an objective to accomplish. Because I was being treated in a not overly hostile manner, I assumed that I was being held by a third party to the conflict, and not by the government against which the strike was directed. I fully realized where I was being held the next day. I was taken, eyes covered, to the hospital to have my injuries examined. I could, however, see through one gap in the Arabic head dress which was wrapped around my eyes. Through that gap I could see the license plates of cars that read SYR726, SYR135, etc. Seeing this made me realize that I was in Syria. During the previous two weeks my area of concentration was centered around the airport compound where our Marines were stationed. I had not kept track of the many various factions in Lebanon and Syria. Keeping track of all of them would have been just too much to follow. It was difficult to determine who the good guys and the bad guys were. It did not hit me completely until about ten days later as I was reading an account of the strike in a copy of a newspaper that was given to me.

In a matter of two to three days my initial feelings of self pity and bitterness dissolved and were replaced by a feeling of confidence and resolve. At one point I thought, "Look, I'm alive, I've got both of my arms and both of my legs. I can see. It's just a matter of time now. Maybe a long time, but it is just a matter of time." This mission was an instrument of foreign policy which was initiated from the top. To be chosen to participate indicates that somebody who is in a position of authority and responsibility had confidence in me and my abilities. When a person in a position of authority expresses confidence in you **it feels good!**

Now I directed my thoughts toward my extended mission of captivity. I had so much time to think that my mind wandered through my experience in SERE School in Brunswich, Maine. This is a school that no naval aviator will forget, and I now know it helped me a great deal. There I learned that the code of conduct is a **personalized** guideline to use to maintain your self dignity. My personal interpretation of the code and my goals were not to incriminate my country, protect what I felt was sensitive information, and that my mission was not over until I was returned to U.S. jurisdiction. On these points I feel that I was successful, but I don't know if I would have been successful if my captivity had lasted for a much longer period of time. The most difficult aspect of my captivity was wondering in my own mind whether or not I was responding to each situation properly. These situations included the questioning sessions and my relations with my captors.

The most frequent question that I am asked is, "How did they treat you?" I can only compare my treatment to what I was trained for, and that was the Vietnam type experience which was much more severe over a much longer period of time. With that as a baseline, I consider that I was treated much better than I or anyone else expected. Many factors contributed to the quality of my treatment. From my point of view, being a black naval officer had some impact. The Syrians do not have a particularly unblemished track record with Israeli POWs. I think that they considered me more of a political prisoner under house arrest than a POW. They knew that I was worth much more as a political carrot. It impresses me that the Syrians chose to follow some basic humanitarian guidelines including extensive medical treatment. I was seen by an English speaking doctor every day for the first two weeks, and taken to the local hospital for X-rays and other treatment. I was allowed to write and receive unsensored letters. My captivity the last three weeks was basically comfortable with no restrictions on my activities inside the room, and there was minimal harrassment after the first four days.

I was amazed by the amount of public recognition and support that I received upon my return to the United States. It was an event that seemed to cross all boundary lines and affect all Americans. There existed some interesting chemistry that I cannot explain and don't fully understand. I received 160,000 Christmas cards. I can't explain what makes an individual in Pennsylvania or Texas take five minutes to write a card that they are not sure will be delivered to someone they have never met and who is an ocean away. That's something special.

Obtaining instant celebrity status can at times be very interesting and fun, but at the same time it can be occasionally difficult to understand and handle. I'm not particularly proud of the fact that I was shot down and unable to accomplish the mission I was sent on. Somehow it doesn't seem right to me that I'm recognized for my failure, when the individuals who were successful remain anonymous. I am proud of the fact that I was in a position to participate in that mission.

Finally, I feel extremely lucky on several accounts. First, I survived a violent ejection in excess of 450 knots that I don't remember. Second, the Syrians felt obligated to treat me in a humane manner, and did at least care for my basic needs. Third, I was released in only thirty days, which at the time seemed to be a year, but in comparison to most POWs or captive senarios is very short. I realize now that there are some increased responsibilities that have been placed on me, and I accept them.

My attitude toward the Navy and my place in it has not changed, and my mental outlook toward what we were trying to accomplish remains steady. After eight months of rehabilitation I was returned to flight status, and that felt good. I know now that if I were asked I would fly that mission again.

MODELER'S SECTION

KIT REVIEWS

Note: It is unfortunate that only three kits have been released of the attack versions of the A-6 Intruder. All are rather old, and are not on a par with the kits being released today. They all represent the A-6A, but since there were no external changes between the A-6A and A-6E, all can be built as an A-6E. Hasegawa has recently re-released its 1/72nd scale kit as an A-6E TRAM, with some new parts, but the kit still needs a lot of work.

Because the Intruder is such a significant aircraft in America's arsenal of naval airpower, we can only hope that new kits will be forthcoming. A kit that is up to today's standards in detailing and accuracy would be welcomed, particularly in 1/72nd and 1/48th scale.

1/100th SCALE KITS

Tamiya A-6A, Kit Number PA 1012

Considering its age and small scale, this is not a bad kit, but it is not a good one either. It is molded in white plastic, and consists of 47 parts. Scribing is a bit on the heavy side, but is generally accurate and represents all of the important control surfaces, panels, and details of the Intruder. Boundary layer fences and wing tip speed brake hinges are a bit thick, as might be expected in this scale, and could be improved by replacing them with thin plastic card. Fuselage speed brakes are separate pieces, and can be displayed in the open or closed position.

The landing gear struts are lacking in detail, which is common in small scales, but it provides sturdy support for the model. It will be wise to add weight in the nose if the model is to sit properly on the tricycle gear. One set of nose gear doors comes as a one-piece closed configuration, and another three-piece set is used if the gear is to be shown extended. There is no nose wheel well. The main gear doors are in two pieces, and may be assembled either open or closed. However, one gear door is missing. The forward main gear doors on the actual aircraft have a lower part in the form of a small door that is hinged to the upper portion. (See pages 18 and 19.) These lower parts of the doors are missing from the kit. Main gear wheels and tires are nice, but the nose wheels leave something to be desired, showing too much wheel and not enough tire. A two-piece stand is provided if the model is to be shown in the in-flight position.

Tamiya was the first to issue the A-6 in 1/100th scale. The model is quite good in most respects.

It would seem that Tamiya had intended to include a tail hook in this kit, because there is a slot for one in the appropriate place. However, there is no hook included in the kit. One will have to be built from scratch. The tail-mounted fuel dump mast and tiedown is represented as part of the fuselage a little too far aft, causing an incorrect outline at the base of the leading edge of the rudder. This is a rather minor point, and will not generally be noticed if not corrected. Wing tips are of the early variety with no ECM gear mounted, nor is there a representation of the earlier AN/ALQ-100 radar deception antennas on the pylons.

The windscreen and canopy come as separate clear pieces, and the framing for the canopy rails and aft fairing is a separate white piece. This allows for the canopy to be positioned in the open position. The framing that is scribed into the windscreen is inaccurate, making the two front portions of the windscreen too narrow. The outer framing is too straight, which compounds the problem. The best solution to this problem is simply to sand and polish off the existing framing, and then repaint the framing on correctly. The cockpit interior is simple, consisting of a single piece with two seats molded in. A decal instrument panel is provided. In order to make this cockpit even close to accurate, it should be rebuilt from scratch. The seats should be offset with a center console between them both horizontally and vertically. Side consoles must also be added. The instrument panel in the kit is flat, while in the actual aircraft it is on several levels. This is easily remedied by using some layers of thin plastic card to build it up. This may be a lot of work for such a small kit, but even in 1/100th scale, the roomy side-by-side cockpit of the Intruder requires detailing. A control column on the pilot's side, and a radar scope and control pedestal on the B/N's side, will complete the basic requirements that will make an adequate cockpit.

Fuel tanks are provided for all five pylons. Those for the wing pylons have a single vertical fin, while the centerline pylon has two fins that are angled at ninety degrees. This is correct, but some centerline tanks have no fins. We recommend using these tanks on all pylons, or using no ordnance at all, since the bombs that are provided in the kit are very bad. The closest thing they resemble is a 750 pound bomb, from the WW-II era, but they do not even represent these well at all. If ordnance is to be used, we suggest scratch-building it, or modifying ordnance from other kits.

General fit of the kit is not as good as it should be, and some filling and sanding will be required, particularly around the intakes, engines, and the panel that forms the underside of the fuselage. With a little work, a TRAM turret, air scoop, and exhaust for aft avionics bay cooling can be added. A straight -E can be built right from the box, but in either case, decals will have to be found, and that won't be easy. Decals available in this kit, and in the Revell re-release, are listed in the Decal Listing at the end of this section of the book, but no other decals exist for the Intruder in 1/100th scale. The decals provided in these two kits are all representative of squadron markings carried on early Intruders during their deployments in Vietnam. The modeler is therefore limited to the decals provided in these two kits unless he wants to do some artwork of his own.

Revell A-6A, Kit Number 4025

This is an identical re-release of the Tamiya kit covered above. The only changes are the decals, the box, and the instruction sheet.

Revell reissued the Tamiya 1/100th scale kit in 1985.

1/72nd SCALE KITS

Hasegawa A-6A, Kit Numbers JS-023, 023, 1023, & E006

All of these kits are simply re-releases of a basic A-6A Intruder, and as such will be reviewed together here. The only differences are the decals (covered in the Decal Listing), box art, and instruction sheets. Kit JS-023 was molded in white plastic, the others were molded in light gray. All but E006 also carry the Minicraft label, being issued by Minicraft when they distributed the Hasegawa line in the United States.

If you build in 1/72nd scale, you build this kit or its updated cousin (reviewed next), or you don't build an Intruder. It is very difficult to believe that this is the only 1/72nd scale kit ever developed of such an important combat aircraft. With its use in Vietnam, and its more recent exploits over Lebanon and Libya, it seems that some other company would issue an updated kit that is up to today's standards in modelmaking. Perhaps Fujimi or ESCI will soon add the Intruder variants to their recent excellent releases in 1/72nd scale.

Molding of the parts is not as good as one might expect. There is flash to remove, and a bit of work will have to be done with a knife and sandpaper in order to get some of the parts to fit well. But the outline is generally good, and the raised surface scribing is not overstated. It shows most Intruder surface features rather nicely, but does miss a few. Noticeable are the holes in the fuselage speed brakes. These are not holes at all, but are simply scribed circles. This may work out for the best though, because if you desire to build the model as one of the earlier aircraft that had the holes in the speed brakes (before or after they were bolted shut) you simply need to drill the holes out where indicated by the scribed circles. If you plan to build an A-6 without the speed brake holes, then you only need to sand off the scribed circles. If these fuselage brakes are to be shown open, then it is best to rework the interiors of the wells since they are not accurate.

The tail hook consists of only the hook portion and the part just above the hook itself. The "Y" part is not included. This is not too bad if an earlier Intruder is to be modeled. Originally this upper "Y" portion had covering that was flush with the underside of the fuselage when the hook was up. Only the end of the hook was then visible, and that is what you have with this kit. However, there are still two problems. First, the hook is not shaped very well, and should be redone from scratch, and second, there is no well for the hook. Once assembled, you can see around the sides of it up into the hollow fuselage unless this is covered by sheet plastic.

The horizontal tail is another problem. It is the type with the elevator as used on only the very first Intruders. The scribing for the elevator should be filled in so as to make the tail plane look like the proper "all flying" type.

Like the rest of the kit, the landing gear is not cleanly molded and lacks detail. There is no nose gear well, and the wells for the main gear are not detailed. The forward main gear doors do not fit together well, and will have to be filled and sanded at their hinge points while leaving the proper gap between the lower doors. The wheels and tires are not as bad as the doors, struts, and wells. Generally, with a little reworking, detailing, and patience, the landing gear can be

These photographs show an early release of the Hasegawa kit built with a lot of extra detailing added. The slats, flaps, spoilers and speed brakes have all been opened up, and the interior surfaces are painted red. This adds a lot of color to the model. The canopy has been opened, and the cockpit detailed. The left side boarding ladder has been opened. With some of the more colorful markings available in decal form for this kit, it can be built into a very colorful and appealing model if the builder is willing to take the time and effort.

improved significantly.

External stores consist of fuel tanks for the centerline and inboard wing stations. However, the cutouts that should be on the trailing edge of the flaps above the end of the pylon tanks are not present. They can easily be added with a knife and a file. For the outboard pylons, MERs and bombs are provided. These lack detail, and we recommend replacing them with those from the Hasegawa 1/72nd scale weapons kits. Weapons Set 1 will supply better MERs and bombs, while Weapons Sets 2, 3, and 4, will provide other ordnance that can be substituted for the MERs and bombs.

The cockpit will need a lot of work too. The instrument panel is flat, not having the proper stepped levels. There is no detailing except for some scribed lines, and with the various scopes and displays that need to be represented, the modeler has a lot of scratch work to do. Another cockpit piece is the floor and seat combination. The seats are not

staggered as they should be, are missing their upper headrests, and have no detailing. These should be replaced. A center horizontal console is between them, but there is no vertical console or side consoles. There is no control column on the pilot's side, nor radar controls for the B/N's side. The area behind the seats has no detailing except for a single box-like affair molded into the fuselage halves. This will have to be removed, and the entire area reworked. The best thing to do is just start over and build the cockpit from scratch.

The canopy/windscreen combination is perhaps the worst part of the kit. It is split lengthwise into two parts. It must be glued together, then assembled to the model. Fit around the forward portion of the windscreen where it joins the radome is very poor, and will require a lot of filling, sanding, and polishing in order to provide a satisfactory result. The other particularly bad fit is the under-fuselage piece, but this is a very difficult shape to reproduce in plastic parts when molding considerations are taken into account. It's a problem area on all Intruder kits.

Being modeled after an early Intruder, the kit has no ECM antennas. The earlier AN/ALQ-100 antennas are not present, nor are the later fairings under the wing tips. In most cases, one of the two will probably have to be added. The engine intakes and exhausts as well as several smaller intakes in various places on the model will look better if opened up. The small scoop, located just below the canopy on the right side, is missing and should be added. The model can be made even more attractive if the slats, flaps, spoilers, and speed brakes on the wings are opened up, but that is a lot of work, and will require using wings from two kits in order to do it right.

This is a lot of criticism for this kit, but it is over twenty years old, so some of it is to be expected. The basic shape is correct, so the main thing it needs is some detailing. By using the photos and drawings in this book, an accurate and detailed model can be built. It will just take a little patience, a lot of time, and some scratch building on the part of the modeler.

Hasegawa A-6E TRAM, Kit Number 709

This is the best kit of the Intruder to use if a model of any but the earliest A-6 test aircraft is to be built. The reason for this is that when Hasegawa re-released this kit as an A-6E TRAM, it also made some other improvements over the other issues covered above. These improvements will save the modeler a lot of work having to make them himself. They include an all new tail hook piece that includes the entire hook molded in the raised position. The entire hook is visible as it has been on the actual aircraft for many years. The small air scoop just below the right side of the canopy has been added to the fuselage, and ECM fairings have been added to the wing tips. The cutouts in the flaps for the fuel tanks have also been added. The horizontal tail has been changed to the "all flying" type.

Of course the most evident change is the addition of the TRAM turret and extra intake scoop for the aft fuselage. An exhaust hole for the aft cooling system has been molded into the fuselage, but Hasegawa missed the change that eliminated the lower beacon light from the forward nose gear door. This should be removed, and a new pair of lights added under the intakes.

If you choose to build an A-6A, simply delete the TRAM turret and scoop, and fill the exhaust hole. If necessary for the aircraft you are modeling, remove the ECM antennas from the wing tips. Add the AN/ALQ-100 if necessary. If the ECM fairings are not needed on the wing tips, it may be best to use the wings from one of the earlier releases, but don't forget to add the cutouts above the external fuel tank locations for the inboard pylons.

Although there were some improvements a lot of problems still remain. The MERs and bombs are the same as before, and no improvements have been made to the land-

The latest reissue of the Hasegawa kit has been updated to the A-6E TRAM configuration.

ing gear. The poor canopy remains the same as before, as does the cockpit. The decals provide formation light panels for the fuselage sides just above the engine exhausts, but the older small light is still scribed into the plastic. Be sure to fill it in if the formation light panel is to be used.

With a number of improvements over the older releases, this is the better of the 1/72nd scale releases to begin with. But a lot of work is in store for the modeler in order to produce a good finished product. Be prepared to spend a long time at your bench with this book in hand. By the time you finish building all of the details yourself, you will be a much more experienced modeler!

1/48th SCALE KITS

Fujimi A-6A, Kit Number 0777

This, along with the Testors re-release, is the only version of the attack versions of the Intruder available in 1/48th scale. It is quite dated, and shows its age, though not as badly as the earlier Hasegawa releases. The model is molded in white plastic, and is nicely scribed, although light rivets are present with the scribing, and these should be removed. The only problem is that when the rivets are sanded off, the scribing tends to go with them, and needs to be replaced.

As with the Hasegawa kits, this kit provides the basis for building a good model of the Intruder if the modeler is willing to add a lot of the detailing that just was not present in models when this one was released. There are some areas where the outline is not as good as it should be, but these would be hard to do anything about, and are best left alone. From the age standpoint, the model lacks any ECM fit, so these will have to be added as appropriate for the specific aircraft being modeled. The small scoop just below the right side of the canopy is likewise missing, and should be added. The speed brakes on the fuselage are the original versions with the holes, but these can easily be filled if desired.

The cockpit has some detailing, but most of it is wrong. While the seats are staggered, they are very poor, and could be rebuilt, or ones from F-14 kits could be used as a basis with some reworking and fitting. The center horizontal console is present, but the vertical console and side consoles are missing. The instrument panel has a scope hood on it for the B/N, and a number of raised circles represent instruments. However, they are not even an approximation of what the instruments in any A-6 looked like. The very noticeable scope on the pilot's side is not even represented. The best thing to do is start over and build an accurate instrument panel. A very inadequate control column is the only other detail in the cockpit proper. The area behind the seats is "busy" with some plumbing and a slot for a phony vertical slide extending up to the canopy. This was to provide one of those "working features" popular with kits twenty years ago. Forget using the slide, and build the model with the canopy open or closed as desired. The canopy itself is a three-piece affair, and is much better than the one in the Hasegawa kit. But again, watch the fit between the windscreen and the radome. Study the photos in this book, and detail out the area behind the seats (as well as the rest of the cockpit) yourself. The results will be much better and well worth it.

The landing gear is not too bad, and provides a sturdy base for this rather large model. But again, it's the detailing that is required, and will have to be added by the modeler, particularly in the wells. The tail hook is the older covered type, and a new one will have to be made in most cases in order for it to look like the real thing.

External stores include centerline and wing fuel tanks, and three sizes of rather generic-looking bombs. The smaller bombs are to go on multiple ejector racks, while the larger bombs attach directly to the pylons. Two Bullpup missiles are also included. As with the Hasegawa kit, we recommend using the Hasegawa weapons sets to replace the MERs and bombs in this kit. The external fuel tanks, and perhaps the Bullpup missiles, are the only stores that come in the kit that we would recommend using. If the Bullpups are to be used, then a launch rail will have to be fabricated from plastic card stock. The missiles did not attach directly to the pylons as the kit has them.

It would be a rather simple task to add a TRAM turret and air scoop to this model to bring it up to TRAM standards. The aft air conditioning exhaust, ECM fit, and changed lower beacon light would all be rather simple compared to the detailing job that is required in order to make this a good representation of an A-6. But so far it is the only game in town, and until someone like Monogram produces a new updated A-6 kit, a lot of work will have to be done by the modeler in order to produce an acceptable 1/48th scale Intruder. With the Intruder's use in Libya, and considering there is almost no competition, it would seem that a new A-6 Intruder kit would be very successful. Hopefully there will be one soon!

Testors A-6A, Kit Number 333

The kit is molded in light gray plastic. There is a different box, new decals, and a different instruction sheet. Otherwise this kit is identical to the Fujimi kit reviewed above. The decals that are included are in the Decal Listing.

Fujimi issued the first 1/48th scale model of the A-6. It is rather old and not up to the standards of present day 1/48th scale kits produced by most companies.

Testors re-released the Fujimi A-6 kit in 1984. There were no changes except for the decals and the box.

CONVERSION KIT AND ACCESSORIES

Maquettes Dauzie 1/72nd Scale Conversion Kit 72 004

There is no kit of a KA-6D tanker available in any scale. While it would be a relatively simple task to convert one of the standard A-6 models to a tanker, Maquettes Dauzie in France has released a conversion kit that provides a under-fuselage piece for the Hasegawa 1/72nd scale kit. It fits into the fuselage just ahead of the tail hook, and includes the fairing for the in-flight refueling drogue. It is nicely molded out of a resin-type material, and greatly simplies the conversion to a tanker. The kit is primarily for building an EA-6A, and will be reviewed further in the Detail & Scale volume on the EA-6A and EA-6B. For further information, modelers should write to their distributors: TRAME, 9 Rue Mayer, 75006 Paris, France.

Maquettes Dauzie 1/72nd Scale U.S. Navy Tow Tractors, Kits 72 006 and 72 007

These two kits in 1/72nd scale provide U.S. Navy tow tractors for use in dioramas featuring the Intruder or any other Navy aircraft. Kit 72 006 is of a tractor with the auxiliary power unit, while 72 007 is the tractor alone. The models are cast in the same resin-like material mentioned in the conversion kit review at left, and have metal hooks. Kit 72 006 also provides wire for a power hook-up, and the compressed air hose. They are very nicely done, and information about them can be obtained from the address given at left.

DECAL LISTING

KIT DECALS							
Kit	Scale	Type	Number	Unit	Tail Code	Scheme	Comments
Tamiya PA 1012	1/100	A-6A	152926	VA-65	NH	Gray/White	Tail code and markings used by VA-65 during tour in SEA aboard USS KITTY HAWK
		A-6A	152623	VA-196	NK	Gray/White	USS CONSTELLATION, SEA tour.
		A-6A	151589	VA-75	AG	Gray/White	USS INDEPENDENCE
Revell 4025	1/100	A-6A	155581	VA-65	NH	Gray/White	Tail code and markings used by VA-65 during tour in SEA aboard USS KITTY HAWK
Hasegawa JS-023	1/72	A-6A	152939	VA-35	NG	Gray/White	USS ENTERPRISE
		A-6A	152626	VA-196	NK	Gray/White	USS CONSTELLATION
Hasegawa 023 and E006	1/72	A-6A	158531	VA-65	AG	Gray/White	CAG aircraft, but with no special markings
		A-6A	155704	VA-115	NF	Gray/White	CAG aircraft, USS MIDWAY
Hasegawa 1023	1/72	A-6A	159178	VMA(AW)-322	EA	Gray/White	
Hasegawa 709	1/72	A-6E TRAM	160996	VA-35	AJ	Gray/White	USS NIMITZ, low visibility markings
		A-6E	161671	VMA(AW)-322	EA	Tactical	
Fujimi 0777	1/48	A-6A	152944	VA-35	NG	Gray/White	USS ENTERPRISE
		A-6A	151785	VA-85	NH	Gray/White	USS KITTY HAWK, tail code and markings used during SEA tour
		A-6A	152623	VA-196	NK	Gray/White	USS CONSTELLATION, SEA tour
Testors 333	1/48	A-6A	151785	VA-85	NH	Gray/White	USS KITTY HAWK, tail codes and markings used during SEA tour
		A-6A	155585	VMA(AW)-533	ED	Gray/White	

DECAL SHEETS							
Manufacturer and Sheet Number	Scale	Type	Number	Unit	Tail Code	Scheme	Comments
Microscale 72-79	1/72	A-6A	155624	VMA(AW)-242	DT	Gray/White	Two EA-6A schemes are also included
		A-6A	155692	VMA(AW)-533	ED	Gray/White	
72-80	1/72	A-6A	152623	VA-196	NK	Gray/White	USS CONSTELLATION, SEA cruise
		A-6A	149479	VA-42	AD	Gray/White	
		A-6A	152926	VA-75	NH	Gray/White	USS KITTY HAWK, SEA cruise
		A-6A	151785	VA-85	NH	Gray/White	USS KITTY HAWK, SEA cruise
72-128	1/72	A-6A	154144	VA-52	NL	Gray/White	USS CORAL SEA
		A-6A	155715	VA-115	NF	Gray/White	USS MIDWAY
		A-6E	158532	VA-65	AG	Gray/White	
		A-6A	152954	VA-95	NL	Gray/White	USS CORAL SEA

Manufacturer and Sheet Number	Scale	Type	Number	Unit	Tail Code	Scheme	Comments
Microscale 72-222	1/72	A-6E	159178	VMA(AW)-332	EA	Gray/White	
		A-6A	149949	VMA(AW)-242	DT	Gray/White	
		A-6A	155652	VMA(AW)-224	WK	Gray/White	
		A-6E	152607	VMA(AW)-224	WK	Gray/White	
		A-6E	155637	VMA(AW)-121	VK	Gray/White	
72-299	1/72	A-6E	152587	VA-75	AC	Gray/White	USS SARATOGA, A-7A and EA-6B also included
72-302	1/72	A-6E	155307	VA-145	NE	Gray/White	USS RANGER, RA-5C and F9F-5 also included
72-413	1/72	A-6E	155689	VMA(AW)-121	VK	Tactical	Low-visibility markings, Two F-18s also included
		A-6A	159180	VMA(AW)-332	EA	Gray/White	
72-428	1/72	A-6A	155585	VMA(AW)-533	ED	Gray/White	
		A-6A	154140	VA-115	NF	Gray/White	USS MIDWAY, one EA-6A also included
72-429	1/72	A-6E	155712	VA-145	NE	Gray/White	USS RANGER
		KA-6D	152894	VA-196	NK	Gray/White	USS ENTERPRISE
		A-6A	152634	VA-128	NJ	Gray/White	
72-493	1/72	A-6A	155600	VA-196	NK	Gray/White	USS ENTERPRISE, one F8U-1 and one AD-6 also included
72-495	1/72	A-6E	160425	VA-196	NK	Gray/White	USS CORAL SEA, two F-4Ns also included
72-535	1/72	A-6E TRAM	159904	VA-95	NH	Tactical	Very poor painting instructions - no top views. No mention is made that these are TRAM aircraft. VA-95 & VA-35 aircraft are switched on instructions.
		A-6E TRAM	159317	VA-35	AJ	Tactical	
		A-6E TRAM	155694	VMA(AW)-533	AA	Tactical	
48-9	1/48	A-6A	155585	VMA(AW)-533	ED	Gray/White	
		A-6A	154140	VA-115	NF	Gray/White	USS MIDWAY, one EA-6A also included
48-48	1/48	A-6E	155712	VA-145	NE	Gray/White	USS RANGER
		KA-6D	152894	VA-196	NK	Gray/White	USS ENTERPRISE
		A-6A	152634	VA-128	NJ	Gray/White	
48-91	1/48	A-6A	155692	VMA(AW)-533	ED	Gray/White	
		A-6E	159178	VMA(AW)-332	EA	Gray/White	
		A-6E	152607	VMA(AW)-224	WK	Gray/White	
48-187	1/48	A-6E	155689	VMA(AW)-121	VK	Tactical	
		A-6E	159180	VMA(AW)-332	EA	Gray/White	
48-225	1/48	A-6E	158532	VA-65	AG	Gray/White	
		A-6A	154144	VA-52	NL	Gray/White	USS CORAL SEA
48-234	1/48	A-6A	152954	VA-95	NL	Gray/White	USS CORAL SEA
		A-6A	155715	VA-115	NF	Gray/White	USS MIDWAY
48-270	1/48	A-6E	152621	VA-95	NH	Gray/White	USS AMERICA, one F-4J also included
48-271	1/48	A-6E	160425	VA-196	NK	Gray/White	USS CORAL SEA, two F-4N's also included
48-273	1/48	A-6A	155600	VA-196	NK	Gray/White	USS ENTERPRISE, one F8U-1 and one AD-6 also included
48-309	1/48	A-6E TRAM	161086	VA-42	AD	Tactical	Very poor painting instructions -- no top views. No mention is made that these are TRAM aircraft that require conversion.
		A-6E TRAM	159315	VA-55	AK	Tactical	
		A-6E TRAM	157025	VA-176	AE	Tactical	
48-310	1/48	A-6E TRAM	159904	VA-95	NH	Tactical	Very poor painting instructions. No info on TRAM conversion is given nor is it even mentioned that these are TRAM aircraft. VA-95 and VA-35 aircraft are switched on instructions.
		A-6E TRAM	159317	VA-35	AJ	Tactical	
		A-6E TRAM	155694	VMA(AW)-533	AA	Tactical	

This listing includes all readily available decals for the A-6 bomber and tanker versions as of press time for this book, September 1986. We urge modelers to get as much reference material as possible on the actual aircraft they are modeling before using these decals. In many cases instructions are in error or are very incomplete.